# WALKS THROUGH HISTORY
# KENT

# WALKS THROUGH HISTORY
# KENT

## John Wilks

First published in Great Britain in 1998 by
The Breedon Books Publishing Company Limited
Breedon House, 3 The Parker Centre,
Derby, DE21 4SZ.

This edition published in Great Britain in 2012 by The Derby Books
Publishing Company Limited, 3 The Parker Centre, Derby, DE21 4SZ.

ISBN 978-1-78091-179-3

# Contents

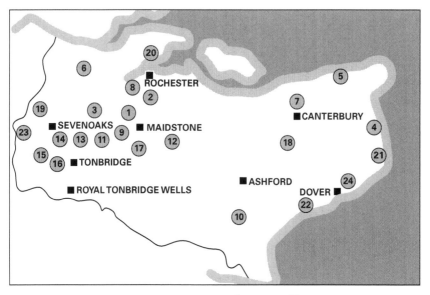

# Key map to the walks

# A brief historical introduction

Each walk in this book has been chosen not only because it is a pleasant walk in its own right, but also because it goes past sites which reveal the rich and varied history of the county. The walks are arranged chronologically, each walk having a major historical theme, and together they take the walker through 4,000 years of Kentish history. The purpose of this introduction is to show how each of the walks in this collection fits into the overall history of the county, a history that is very much shaped by Kent's proximity to Europe. For through migration, trade and invasion, Kent has had close contact with the Continent throughout its history.

In prehistoric times Britain was connected to continental Europe by a land bridge. It was across this bridge that Homo Sapiens first reached Britain, entering through its southeastern corner and gradually spreading north and west. Human remains and flint tools 200,000 years old have been found at Swanscombe near Gravesend, the earliest example of Kentish man. Britain only became an island around 6500BC, when the seas rose and flooded what is now the English Channel, breaking through the Straits of Dover. Initially this drastically reduced the rate of migration from the Continent, but gradually man perfected the building of canoes and leather-made boats, small craft that were nevertheless sturdy enough to allow him to cross the treacherous seas of the channel.

These early Stone Age men lived mainly in the open air, camping beside rivers and lakes and existing on what could be hunted or gathered. Consequently, they made little mark upon the landscape. Occasionally they used caves for temporary shelter, and evidence has been found in one such cave, at Oldbury Hill, (walk 3) that it was regularly used by hunters for seasonal refuge about 2001BC. But although the dwellings they built may have made no mark on the landscape, the tombs and trackways made by Stone Age man are still to be seen today. Collective tombs known as long barrows can be seen at the Coldrum Stones (walk 1) and at Kits Coty (walk 2). These tombs have more in common in their construction with Holland and Denmark than with the rest of Britain, evidence that there was regular contact across the seas. The ancient trackways of these people can still be followed, running for instance along the foot of the North Downs (walk 2).

During the Stone Age the population was very small and widely scattered, with between 10,000 and 20,000 people in the whole of Britain. Improved agricultural techniques and the use of metal for tools led to a rapid population expansion during the Bronze Age (2000BC to 700BC), and man became organised into tribes or clans. Burial was now by cremation, with the ashes interred in round barrows (walk 10). When climatic changes rendered large areas of the uplands and the north of the island uninhabitable, pressure upon the remaining land made inter-tribal conflict inevitable, with the new metal technology being pressed into service to provide weapons.

By the Iron Age, about 700BC onwards, Britain had regular contact with Europe, exporting corn, cattle, hides, gold, silver, iron, hunting dogs and slaves. The bulk of this trade was through Kent, already known by that name and already the most prosperous part of Britain. Towards the end of this period Kent was settled by the Belgae, a continental tribe driven from their homelands in Gaul (modern France and Belgium) by the increasing power of the Roman Empire. This powerful and warlike tribe built hilltop strongholds such as Oldbury Hill Fort (walk 3), for use in times of emergency, and maintained strong links with their continental cousins, both in terms of trade and militarily. By the middle of the first century BC, British mercenaries were fighting in Gaul against the Romans, and Britain was sanctuary to Rome's enemies.

The actions of the Belgae and other hostile tribes eventually provoked Roman intervention. Julius Caesar came twice to Britain, firstly in 551BC for a reconnaissance, then again in 541BC, this time with a much stronger force with which to subdue Rome's most prominent enemies. On both occasions Caesar landed in the vicinity of present day Deal (walk 21), the closest point to continental Europe where the flat open beaches offered easy landing. Caesar declared that Kent was the most civilised part of Britain, easily on a par with Gaul, and planted the seeds for Britain's incorporation into the Roman Empire. A century later Rome returned, this time bent upon the permanent occupation of Britain. An invading army landed at Pegwell Bay (walk 4), swept up through Kent, and overcame a British army at the Battle of the Medway (walk 8). Although the eventual subjugation of the whole of England 'would take many years, resistance in Kent was at an end, and for the next four centuries Kent reaped the benefits of being part of the Roman Empire. The Romans made Richborough their major British port (walk 4) and trade between Britain and the Continent flowed through Richborough and across Kent along the Roman road of Watling Street. Cities like Rochester and Canterbury and luxurious villas such as that at Lullingstone followed (walk 6). Initially citizens from the rest of the Empire came to Britain as soldiers, administrators and merchants, but gradually the local population took on Roman values and played an increasing role in the running of the province. A new Romano-British civilisation developed.

By the fourth century the survival of the Roman Empire was under threat. In Britain, Saxon pirates harassed the coastline. To counter this a series of strongpoints, the Forts of the Saxon Coast, were built, at such places as Richborough (walk 4) and Reculver (walk 5). Eventually, however, the Romans were forced to evacuate Britain in 410AD, and Kent was increasingly prey to the influx of warring bands of Saxons, Jutes, and Danes. The Saxon warlords Hengist and Horsa made the Isle of Thanet their base, from which they established the Saxon kingdom of Kent. Although Romano-British civilisation continued, Britain gradually reverted to a rurally-based tribal society. Political and economic control was increasingly in the hands of a landowning aristocracy, who were under little central control from a king. During this time Kent still remained relatively wealthy and reasonably civilised. The culture inherited from the Romans was not swept away, but forced underground.

Christianity had been imposed upon Britain by Emperor Constantine in the fourth century AD but was lost as a national religion when the Germanic tribes arrived, bringing their own religious beliefs. In 597 AD Pope Gregory sent St Augustine to Britain to convert the country back to Christianity. Augustine landed at Ebbsfleet and journeyed to the Kentish capital, Canterbury, where he was welcomed by King Ethelbert and his Christian Queen, Bertha. The King and his subjects rapidly converted to the returned religion, and Augustine established the Archbishopric of Canterbury as a jumping-off ground for the further spread of Christianity (walk 7).

From the eighth to the 10th centuries Kent, along with much of the rest of England, was increasingly harried by the Danes, until they were finally driven away by King Alfred. (The site of one of Alfred's campaigns can be seen near Appledore on walk 10.) Kent was soon incorporated into the Saxon kingdom of England and enjoyed a return to peace and prosperity. Settlements expanded further and further into the huge Wealdan Forest, which covered much of the interior of the county. Towns grew in size and wealth, and trade with Europe was re-established. There is little direct evidence of the Saxon period to be seen today. The Saxons only occasionally built castles (such as Leeds Castle, walk 12), and most of their churches and palaces have been incorporated into later buildings. However, many of the settlements in Kent date from this era, and their Saxon origins are denoted in placenames: the ending 'den' and 'ing' mean an enclosure, 'ley' refers to a clearing in the forest, 'ham' and 'ton' denote farms and dwellings.

In 1066 William, Duke of Normandy, invaded Britain with a small army, bent upon securing the English crown to which he had at least some legitimate claim. Unlike previous invaders, William did not land in Kent but in neighbouring Sussex. After defeating the English at Hastings, William's army marched around the coast of Kent, receiving reinforcements from Normandy en route, and marched up Whatling Street to London to receive his crown.

William's immediate need after the Battle of Hastings had overthrown the old Anglo-Saxon monarchy was to ensure that the population were subdued and that any revolts were nipped in the bud, and also to ensure that no other adventurer was able to invade from abroad. William saw to it that a castle was built in every county, town, and at points of strategic importance. The great castles at Rochester (walk 8) and Dover (walk 24) were started at this time.

The Normans brought with them the art of castle building to England. William gave his nobles a free hand to build private castles to defend their lands. In the years immediately following the conquest a rash of castles sprang up over England, a visible reminder to a cowed population of the power of their new masters. The initial castles were simple affairs, an earth mound with a simple wooden keep on top and a wooden palisade around the outside, known as 'motte and bailey'. Soon, however, these were replaced by more substantial stone-built castles, which provided bases of wealth and power (examples are seen at Eynsford castle, walk 6, and Leeds Castle, walk 12).

The Norman Conquest was essentially an aristocratic one and did not result in any mass influx of new settlers into England. Only 6,000 men accompanied William to England. William needed an army to defend his conquest and a nobility who could be guaranteed to defend his new kingdom. He achieved both these goals by taking the land of the defeated Saxon aristocracy and parcelling it out to his supporters, in return for which they were obliged to provide knights and men-at-arms when required. This system of rights and obligations based upon land tenure is known as feudalism. These Norman landowners, churchmen as well as secular barons, now had a vested interest in defending their new estates, and through them the integrity of the realm. The effects of the introduction of feudalism can be seen on the ground in West Malling and Offham (walk 9).

For the Normans, religion was as important as the sword. William was accompanied by his supporter Bishop Lanfranc, who was soon made Archbishop of Canterbury and the foremost churchman in England. During this early Norman period many Saxon religious buildings were extended or rebuilt in the Norman style. The great cathedrals of Canterbury (walk 7) and Rochester (walk 8) date from this time, as did many of Kent's fine old churches, monasteries and abbeys. (Both the church and abbey in West Malling, walk 9, date from this era.) The boundaries between church and state, between obligations and duties owed to and by each, were blurred during the Norman period. This culminated in the great conflict between King Henry II and his Archbishop Thomas Becket, which resulted in the murder of the latter in 1170 in Canterbury Cathedral, and Canterbury thus becoming a place of pilgrimage (walk 7).

The three centuries following the Norman Conquest were a period of consolidation. The Norman kings and barons had great holdings in land on both sides of the channel. While they developed the resources of their new holdings in Britain, they also continued to manage their old ones on the Continent, and in the process forged firm links of trade and travel between the two lands. This was also a time when the new relationship between the king and his barons was hammered out, for William had imposed the new concept that all land belonged to the king, to be given to his subjects in return for service. This view was alien to the established view that the king was only the first among his peers, and on several occasions the nobility resorted to arms against the encroachment of royal power. In 1216 the barons, aided by the French monarchy, revolted against King John, and Dover, Canterbury (walk 7) and Rochester Castles were all involved in the conflict. 1264 saw another Baronial revolt, this time led by Simon de Montefort against Henry III, and again Rochester Castle saw action (walk 8).

Apart from these large scale revolts against royal power by the nobility, there was often fighting whenever the king was weak, either with the nobility fighting each other or fighting their king as they jockeyed for position. Leeds Castle saw an example of one such comparatively minor skirmish in the reign of Edward II (walk 12). Kent was little involved in the last major conflict between the nobles, the Wars of the Roses, which largely ended with the accession of the House of Tudor in 1485.

By the 14th century Kent was the richest county in the land. Money poured in from pilgrims coming to Canterbury (walk 7), rich agricultural land abounded around the margins of the ever-receding forest, and the ports of the channel coast grew powerful and affluent as trade flowed between England and the Continent. Examples of this are seen at Sandwich (walk 4) and Appledore (walk 10). This was not to say Kent was peaceable: the interior of the county was still covered by the Forest of the Weald, settlements were still scattered and the roads between them were poor. Landowners who sought estates in the forest margin often had to fight to impose the law that enabled them to maintain those lands. The dangerous times these lesser landlords lived in is amply demonstrated by the existence of fortified manor houses across the county, such as Old Soar (walk 11) and Ightham Mote (walk 13).

The growing wealth of Kent was not bought without paying the price of social injustice. Feudalism continued to exist until well into the 15th century, and the peasants resented the numerous taxes and arbitrary fines that were imposed upon them without any redress. In 1381 this resentment spilled over as the Peasants Revolt. This started in Essex and in Kent, where the rebels under Wat Tyler attacked local landlords in places such as Appledore (walk 10), before capturing Canterbury Castle (walk 7) and marching upon London. Only after the rebels received promises of reform from young King Richard II did they disperse, only to see those promises rapidly broken and their leaders executed. In 1453 there was another revolt in Kent against the corruption and arbitrary exercise of power by the ruling classes, this time among the more well-to-do commoners. Led by Jack Cade they defeated a royal army at Sevenoaks (walk

14) and occupied London, before again being betrayed by broken royal promises.

During the 14th century Edward III allowed Flemish weavers who were fleeing from religious persecution to settle in Kent, bringing with them the skills needed to start a cloth industry. The villages and towns of the Weald flourished, raising sheep, weaving wool and digging the clay necessary for cleaning and dying the wool. The ports of the channel coast flourished as cloth swelled English exports, and organised themselves into a powerful league known as the Cinque Ports. In return for favourable import-export rights and tax concessions, the Cinque Ports supplied the monarch with ships in times of war and policed the collection of customs duties. Originally the Cinque Ports comprised the four Kentish ports of Dover, Sandwich (walk 4), Romney and Hythe, and Hastings in neighbouring Sussex, but they eventually incorporated another 20 ports along the channel coast. These included some such as Appledore (walk 10), which today are miles from the sea thanks to changes in the coastline.

Iron had been smelted in the Weald since Roman times, but it was initially of poor quality. The invention of water-driven smelting machinery changed this, and in the 16th century Kent became the industrial heart of England. Local iron was mined and smelted using the power of local streams and foundries burning charcoal from the Wealdan Forest. This Kentish iron was forged into tools and weapons that were in high demand in England and abroad. Traces of this industry can still be seen today at West Peckham (walk 17). Many towns in the Weald grew in importance and remained so until the technological developments of the late 18th century moved the industrial focus of England to the coalfields of the Midlands and the North.

By the middle of the reign of Henry VIII Kent was settled, peaceful and increasingly wealthy. Evidence of this prosperity can still be seen in towns such as Chiddingstone (walk 15), Penshurst (walk 16) and Chilham (walk 18). Better communications with London made Kent a favoured place for the homes of crown servants, who built country houses in the county, such as Lullingstone Castle (walk 6). The Tudor period saw the development and expansion of many huge estates across the county, with fine houses surrounded by extensive parks laid out for recreation and stocked for hunting (walk 14 visits one such estate, Knole House). Two of Henry VIII's wives, Anne Boleyn and Anne of Cleves, occupied Hever Castle (walk 15). Sir Philip Sydney, courtier, poet and soldier, the quintessential Elizabethan man, lived at Penshurst Place (walk 16).

The Civil War in the middle of the 17th century largely passed Kent by. There were minor skirmishes at Deal (walk 21), and there are reminders of the Commonwealth Period around Plaxtol, in the form of a rare commonwealth church (walk 11). Generally, however, the Stuart era in Kent was marked by continued tranquillity, with estates such as Chevening (walk 19) continuing to flourish.

Kent has always been in the front line against invasion from the Continent. The Romans, the Saxons and the Danes all invaded through Kent. The shores of Kent, which have changed their course considerably since Roman times, have been defended for 2,000 years against invasion. The Romans built the forts of the Saxon Coast to protect against Germanic invaders (walks 4 and 5). The Saxons under Alfred fought the Danes in its creeks and inlets (walk 10). The Normans, after entering through neighbouring Sussex, rapidly built strong castles in Kent to defend against future continental incursions. During the Hundred Years War the coast of Kent was raided several times by the French (walk 10). Henry VIII's foreign and religious policy made invasion from France again a possibility, and a line of strong modern castles such as Upnor (walk 20) and Deal (walk 21) were built all around the coastline. Henry's forts were never used in his lifetime, but one of them, Upnor, saw service during wars against the Dutch in the following century (walk 20).

Britain was at war against the French for most of the 18th century, and one of the heroes of that struggle, General James Wolfe, was born at Westerham, and is commemorated there (walk 23). This epic struggle culminated in the wars against the Revolutionary Government and its successor the Emperor Napoleon, from 1792 to 1815. Invasion from France, was once again threatened, with Kent in the front line. To counter this, extensive defences were built along the coastline, most especially the vulnerable area around Romney Marsh. Here the Royal Military Canal (walks 10 and 22) was built behind a line of coastal fortifications (visited at Hythe, walk 22). Deal (walk 21) was one of the major ports in England for the Royal Navy during the 18th and 19th centuries, and also profited from a flourishing trade in smuggling. During World War One the Dover Patrol was vital in keeping open Britain's communications with her army in France (walk 24). England was again threatened with invasion in 1940, and Kent saw a major part of a new type of war, this time one fought in the air during the Battle of Britain (walk 24).

From the cliffs above Dover (walk 24) one can look down at the bustling port, with its busy container terminal, and a constant stream of ferries crossing the channel. Around Hythe (walk 22) there are road signs pointing to the Channel Tunnel. Both are modern reminders of that proximity to Europe which has been a constant theme throughout Kent's history.

# Advice to walkers

All but one of the walks in this collection cross countryside for at least part of their route. Although the terrain is not difficult or dangerous, it can become very wet and slippery in places, especially after a shower of rain, and walking boots or stout shoes are recommended for any of these walks. It is also recommended that you carry waterproofs, since the weather can change quickly even in Kent, and you could easily find yourself some distance away from shelter when the skies open, Remember that on some walks there may be occasional brambles, nettles or crops which scratch, so bear this in mind when deciding whether to walk in shorts. Directions for each walk are given in the text and a sketch map included to give an outline of the route. These sketch maps are not detailed enough to navigate by, and it is strongly recommended that you carry the relevant Ordnance Survey map, in case of difficulties or in case you wish to deviate from the route. The 1:50,000 series is perfectly adequate to walk from. Although all directions are accurate at the time of writing, features do occasionally change: a hedge or tree may disappear, a stile may be replaced by a gate. By comparing the written directions with the OS map it should be perfectly possible to find the correct route even if features have occasionally altered. All routes in this book use public rights of way or permissive footpaths when crossing private land. Again, the OS map will confirm the right of way in case of doubt. If a footpath or bridleway is shown on a current map, it is the duty of the landowner to maintain the route and you have a legal right to use it. However, it is sensible to show discretion and compromise rather than a rigid insistence on your rights: for instance, if at certain times of the year the route across an open field is not obvious or is obscured by crops, it may be better to walk around the perimeter of the field. Consideration for others is key when walking, and at all times remember the Countryside Code laid down by the Countryside Commission:

1. Enjoy the countryside and respect its life and work
2. Guard against all risk of fire
3. Fasten all gates
4. Keep your dogs under close control
5. Keep to public paths across farmland
6. Use gates and stiles to cross fences, hedges and walls
7. Leave livestock, crops and machinery alone
8. Take your litter home
9. Help to keep all water clean
10. Protect wildlife, plants and trees
11. Take special care on country roads
12. Make no unnecessary noise

I have indicated where refreshments can be obtained on each walk. On a number of the walks, refreshments are only available at the beginning or end. It is therefore advisable to carry a snack and, more importantly, something to drink with you, especially on the longer walks. Please note that the mention of the existence of a pub is not necessarily an endorsement of it! Convenient car parking places have been indicated for all walks. At the time of writing, most of these were free and there is adequate parking at most spots indicated. Should you have difficulty it is far better to find a different parking spot and make your way to the start of the walk on foot, rather than causing an obstruction with your car. Most importantly, remember you are visiting a place where other people live. Do not cause inconvenience to local people by parking across access to houses, farms, fields or churches.

WALK 1

# The Coldrum Stones: Long barrows and mediaeval tracks

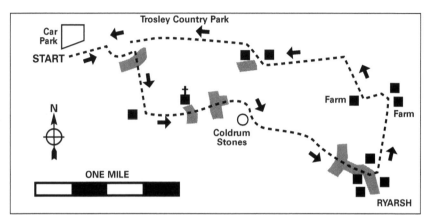

**Distance:** 6 miles

**Map:** OS sheet 177 or 188

**Start and Parking:** The walk starts from Trosley Country Park (grid ref: 633611). This is just to the east of the A227, nine miles south of Gravesend. There is ample car parking there.

**Refreshments:** None

### Historical Background

During the Early and Middle Stone Age, or 'Neolithic' Period (roughly 4000BC to 2500BC), the idea of collective burial was traditional throughout the countries on the western seaboard of Europe. Communities went to huge efforts to build massive communal graves with the primitive tools of the day. These were then used for successive burials over a number of years, being closed and then reopened, until finally they were sealed permanently. The religious significance of this form of burial is not known, nor is it known why some individuals were thus buried but not the rest of the community. It is tempting to speculate that they were leaders of the community, but if so they were perhaps more likely to be religious leaders than political.

These collective tombs are known as barrows, either 'long' or 'round' dependent upon their shape, and are found across the whole of the British Isles and Western Europe. The actual design of the barrow alters according to region. The Coldrum Stones, which are the well-preserved remains of one of the earliest long harrows in Kent, are part of a group called the Medway Barrows. These are far more similar to tombs found in north-west Europe than to tombs found in the rest of Britain, arguing for a strong cultural connection across the North Sea.

## The Walk
**This walk starts in Trosley Country Park and descends the North Downs to visit the Coldrum Stones. It then goes through the pleasant countryside at the foot of the escarpment and returns along part of the Pilgrims' Way.**

- With the toilets and visitors' centre on your left, go down the waymarked path to reach a cross track after a few yards.
- Turn left along the cross track for 350 yards. Ignore a marker for 'Blue Walks' on your right, but 10 yards later, at a post with seven waymarkers on it, turn right and descend steps through trees.
- Ignore side turnings and descend the path, which soon becomes stepped again.
- At the bottom of the steps ignore horse barriers ahead but instead turn left along the path.
- After a quarter of a mile turn right through a horse barrier, at a waymark. Cross a track, pass through another horse barrier, and descend to a lane.
- Cross the lane and enter the field opposite. Keep straight on down the right-hand edge of the field, keeping the fence and trees to your right.
- Pass through a kissing gate and continue straight on along an enclosed footpath. When the path ceases to be enclosed, keep straight on down the right-hand edge of a field.
- Where the fence on the right ends, keep straight on across the field, aiming to the left of houses seen ahead.
- Keep straight on with gardens on the right. When the gardens end, turn left onto a cross track.
- Follow the bottom edge of the field, aiming for a church seen ahead.

*There are fine views of the North Downs on your left. An ancient Neolithic (Stone Age) trackway, later to become used in mediaeval times as the Pilgrims' Way from London to Canterbury, runs along the foot of the Downs. During the Stone Age, the whole of the countryside you are walking through would have been lightly wooded. Even by the Middle Ages, the agricultural land would not have been as extensive as it is today.*

- Pass through a farmyard and into the end of a lane, with the church on your left.

*The main claim to fame of the Church of St Peter and St Paul is an enormous pulpit said to have come from Westminster Abbey, and a collection of human and animal bones exhumed from the Coldrum Long Barrow. The church itself is largely Norman, built by Bishop Gundulph (see walks 8 and 9) around AD1100 on the site of a demolished Saxon church.*

- Walk down the lane. Pass a house on the left after 30 yards and immediately turn left up the slope to a stile.

The Coldrum Long Barrow,
a communal grave from 3000BC.

- Keep straight on across the field, aiming for houses opposite.
- Exit the field into a lane. Cross over the lane and take the tarmacked track opposite, signposted 'Coldrum Long Barrow'.
- Pass through a parking area and continue down the track opposite.
- The track soon narrows into a footpath, passes through trees and emerges into a field. Keep ahead down the right-hand edge of the field. Where the hedge on the right ends, keep ahead over the field.
- Bear right with the path out of the field and down to a cross track. Turn right after 60 yards to Coldrum Long Barrow.

*The Coldrum Long Barrow was a communal grave from the period 3000–2500BC. In structure it was a rectangular earthen mound, orientated roughly east–west, higher at the east where the entrance was. The interior of the tomb consisted of a burial chamber with drystone interior walls, covered with an earthen mound. This in turn was flanked by 24 large blocks of stone (known as sarsen stones), to act as a retaining wall or kerb around the mound. The largest stones flanked the entrance. These sarsen stones are not local in origin. It is possible that they are what are called 'erratic', boulders carried on the glaciers during the Ice Age and deposited many miles from their origin.*

*The construction of the barrow is a type common to tombs in the Medway area, but not found elsewhere in Britain. It is, however, very similar to tombs of the same age found in Western Europe, in particular the Hunebeds of Holland and Germany and the Dysse tombs of Denmark. This is strong evidence that there were close cultural links between the inhabitants of North Kent and those on the Continent, 5,000 years ago.*

*The Coldrum Long Barrow was in use over a considerable period, being opened at successive intervals as fresh corpses were interred. The remains of at least 22 people, of all ages and both sexes, were found inside. The communities who built the barrows were not settled in one place: they would move on every few decades once the land became exhausted. Consequently over time the barrows became further and further away from where the people now lived and required longer and longer journeys to bury the dead in them. This may be the reason why a barrow was eventually permanently sealed and abandoned.*

- Pass the long barrow on your right and continue up the concrete drive for 100 yards. Where the drive turns right, keep straight on down a footpath to a cross track.
- Turn left down the cross track for 25 yards to a field gate between two stiles. Take the stile to the left of the gate and go down the left-hand side of the field, with trees on your left.
- At the end of the trees keep straight on, aiming for a stile in the trees ahead.
- Cross the stile and follow a path through woods to enter scrubland.
- Follow a clear path half-right through scrub land to a stile near the top right-hand corner.
- Cross the stile and turn left along a footpath to cross a footbridge and enter woodland.
- Follow the path as it winds through the wood to reach a lane.
- Turn right in the lane and then immediately turn left down Chapel Street.

- Follow Chapel Street for quarter of a mile to reach houses. Pass the first house on the left, and then immediately turn left up its drive, at a footpath sign. Keep ahead for 20 yards to enter a field.
- Turn left along an enclosed footpath towards the North Downs ridge, with gardens on your left.
- Cross a stile and continue straight on up the right-hand edge of a field.
- At the end of the field, turn right through a gap in the field boundary, then immediately turn left, to continue on the same line of advance, now up the left-hand edge of a field, with a drainage ditch on your left.
- After 100 yards cross a footbridge on the left and continue, now with the ditch on your right, to enter the next field. Continue in the same direction, still with a ditch on your right.
- Where the ditch on the right ends, turn left across the field, aiming for the corner of the wood ahead.
- At the corner of the wood, continue ahead, with the wood on your left. Bear right with the field boundary, then pass through a gap in the hedge on the left at a waymark.
- Turn right in the next field and walk up the right-hand edge, with trees on the right, to a stile.
- Cross the stile and walk up to a drive, in front of a large timber barn. Turn left along the drive, passing a second barn, and follow the drive to a T-junction beside a house on the right.
- Turn left down the drive towards a farm seen ahead. Pass a pumping station on your right, and just before a barn turn right up an enclosed track for quarter of a mile.
- At a T-junction turn left and follow a track, the Pilgrims' Way, for one mile along the foot of the downs. Ignore all turns to the right or left.

*The Pilgrims' Way was the traditional route taken by mediaeval pilgrims travelling from London to Canterbury, to pay homage at the shrine of St Thomas Becket (see walk 7). Pilgrims' used to gather together for protection and travel in groups through countryside that in the 13th century was still forested and lawless. On one side pilgrims would have seen some agricultural land around the villages of Ryarsh and Birling. These would have been huge fields divided into strips and all growing the same crop, with stands of trees between them. On the other side would have been the dark, thick woodland sloping up to the top of the ridge. It is one such group of pilgrims that is immortalised in Chaucer's* Canterbury Tales, *telling tales to pass the time and keep their spirits up.*

*The Pilgrims' Way follows a much older trackway that has followed the foot of the North Downs since Neolithic times, where the chalk of the Downs meets the underlying clay and springs bubble out of the soil. Neolithic man followed this path, with its supply of fresh water, despite the thick forest it ran through. This supports the view that the threat of ambush by ones fellow man was much less then than in later times.*

- The Pilgrims' Way track comes out at the end of a tarmacked road. Turn right between the gates of houses and enter an enclosed track.
- Climb steeply with the track. At the top of the slope, turn sharp left (signposted 'North Downs Way') and pass through a kissing gate beside a horse barrier, marked 'Entrance to Trosley Country Park'.
- Keep ahead along a broad track, ignoring all side turnings, for two thirds of a mile to reach the seven-waymarked post of your outward journey again (but with only four waymarks on this side) at the top of steps down to the left.
- Pass 'Post 3' on the left in 10 yards and follow the track, soon to reach the car park again up on your right.

## WALK 2
# Kits Coty: Stone Age graves and trackways

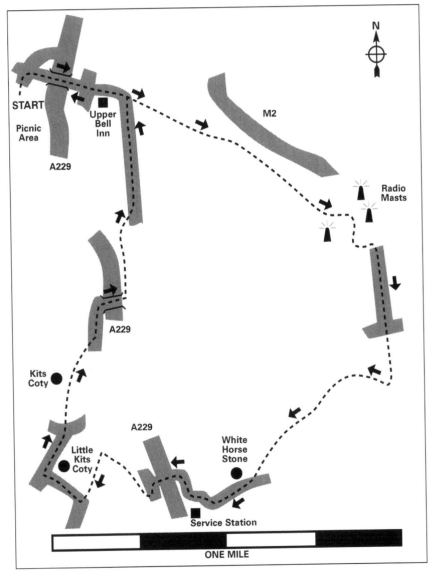

**Distance:** 4 miles
**Map:** OS sheet 178 or 188
**Start and Parking:** The walk commences from Blue Bell Hill Picnic site (grid ref: 743621). Blue Bell Hill is just off the A229 and very close to junction three of the M2, two miles south of Chatham and four miles north of Maidstone. If coming from the south (Maidstone) turn off the A229 just at the summit of the North Downs, following signs for Blue Bell Hill. From the north go to the roundabout where the A229 meets junction two of the M2, and then take a minor road south for half a mile, again signposted Blue Bell Hill. There is parking at the picnic site.
**Refreshments:** Public house at Blue Bell Hill.

### Historical Background

The Stone Age or Neolithic era as a whole lasted from around 4000BC to 2100BC. The people of the Neolithic era had a very sophisticated culture: they lived in settled communities, made and used tools that were suitable for most everyday needs, cultivated the land and herded domesticated animals. They had well-developed religious beliefs and built lasting tombs for certain members of their community, probably those with religious status. Their social organisation was possibly tribal, but more likely based upon an extended family. Because the land was large and the population small (less than 20,000 people in Britain), they had no need for territorial expansion and by and large lived at peace with their neighbours. Their communities were not isolated but had far-reaching communications and limited trade, not only within Britain but abroad as well, and travel, although full of natural hazards, does not seem to have been threatened by their fellow man.

Neolithic people lived in settled but transitory communities. They would clear a patch of the all-pervasive forest, settle and cultivate it for a few years or even a few decades until the land was exhausted and the natural resources of the forest used up, and then move on and start again. Their homes were made of wood and their agricultural methods primitive, and so the only permanent mark they left upon the landscape were their stone and earth-built tombs and their long-distance trackways. That their architectural skills were considerable is demonstrated by the fact that their tombs still survive after 5,000 years: it was not that they could not build homes that were permanent, they simply had no need to.

### The Walk

This walk goes through a region full of evidence of Neolithic man: the flint fields used for tools, the ancient trackways and the two tombs of Kits Coty and Little Kits Coty. It starts on top of the North Downs, descends steeply to travel through the rich arable land on the plain below, and finally re-ascends the ridge.

- From the entrance to the Blue Bell Hill picnic site car park, turn right into the road and after 100 yards cross over the A229 on an elevated road bridge.
- Follow the road to a crossroads at the Upper Bell Inn. Cross over and keep straight on up Mill Lane.

- Where Mill Lane bears right and becomes Warren Road, turn left behind a national speed limit sign to two stiles. Cross the right-most stile into an enclosed path, with a field on the left and stables on the right.
- Follow the enclosed path for 200 yards to reach trees.
- Follow the path through the trees along the edge of a field.
- At the end of the field cross a stile and continue along a clear path leading deeper into the woods. After 50 yards ignore a left turn, and 50 yards further on ignore a cross track and keep straight on, now with the M2 close on your left.
- Where the path emerges into a large field, keep ahead along the left-hand edge of the field, with the M2 still on the left for a short while.

*There are numerous pieces of flint to be seen in this field, a common sight in many fields on the chalk uplands across Britain. Neolithic man made the majority of his tools from flint, and the availability of this valuable commodity was one of the attractions for settling on or near to the chalk ridges of the North and South Downs and the Ridgeway. In some areas of the country there were flint mines, and evidence that tools were mass-produced and traded with other communities. The flint upland here would have been worked just for the immediate needs of the local community.*

- In the far corner of the field, turn right at the foot of a radio mast and continue along the field boundary, passing buildings and another mast on the left.
- Follow the field edge around to a tarmacked drive outside some gates. Turn right along the drive for 300 yards to reach a cross drive.
- Keep straight on over the cross drive and bear half-right along a marked footpath across a large field, aiming for the woods ahead.
- On reaching the woods, turn right along the track, keeping the woods on the left.
- In the corner of the field, where the field boundary turns right, turn left between two sarsen stones and follow the track into the woods.
- Keep straight on at a cross track and follow the path to reach a concrete 'North Downs Way' marker in the middle of a grove of yew trees.

*There is no evidence that yew trees had any religious meaning to Stone Age men, but they did acquire a deep religious significance to man during the Iron Age, 700BC onwards. Deities were to be found in forests and groves, marshes, lakes, rivers and springs. Druids, religious leaders of great power, conducted services in groves, some of which may have been associated with human sacrifice. The yew tree has its blood-red berries fruiting at the time of Midwinter's Day, a time when the world was at its darkest and coldest, and thus had a special significance for ceremonies based around renewing the earth by calling the sun back. Yew trees and their berries became incorporated into the later Christian stories of Christmas.*

- Soon start to descend the spur with the path, with views opening up to the left and then to the right. Ignore a left turn at a fence and continue down the spur, descending ever more steeply, soon using wooden steps set into the bank.

- At the bottom of the steps, turn right with the path and wind through trees for 50 yards to a cross track. Turn left down the cross track and in 30 yards pass through a horse barrier and down a few steps onto a trackway.
- Turn right and follow the trackway.

*From Neolithic times a track has followed the North Downs, not along the summit but along the foot, where the chalk of the Downs meets the underlying clay and springs bubble out of the soil. The supply of fresh water was the reason for Neolithic man following this lower path, despite the thick forest it ran through. This supports the view that the threat of ambush by ones fellow man was much less then than in later times.*

- In 100 yards pass an isolated sarsen stone on your right.

*This stone is called the White Horse Stone, and it appears that it was being transported along the ancient track from the site of its excavation five miles to the east, to where the Kits Coty burial mound was being constructed, a mile west of here. How these huge stones were moved is unknown, but it is likely that ropes were tied around them and they were dragged by a human workforce, either on rollers or more likely using sledges. It is tempting to see the holes at either end of the stone as having been deliberately drilled into the stone to aid pulling, but there is no evidence for this. Why this stone was abandoned is unknown.*

- Follow the trackway around the bottom of a field. Where the track becomes metalled, turn right and walk up towards the service station (being renovated at time of writing) seen ahead.
- Just before the service station, turn right down a metalled cycleway (signposted '17 Rochester') and follow it down and around to the left, to pass through a tunnel under the A229.
- Exit the tunnel and turn left at a T-junction. In 40 yards turn right onto a field path (signed 'North Downs Way')

*This is still the same Neolithic trackway that you were on previously, but it is now called the Pilgrims' Way, used in the Middle Ages by pilgrims bound to Canterbury to worship at the shrine of St Thomas Becket (see walk 7).*

- Follow this tree-lined footpath along the foot of the Downs for quarter of a mile to a cross track. Turn left down the cross track to reach a lane in 200 yards.
- Turn right into the lane and follow it for 350 yards to reach a road.
- Turn right along this busy road for 50 yards to reach Little Kits Coty, keeping an eye open for fast-moving traffic.

*Little Kits Coty was a rectangular burial mound, of the same design as the Coldrum Long Barrow (walk 1). It was orientated roughly east–west, higher at the eastern end, where the entrance is, and sloping down away from the entrance. It had a single communal burial chamber lined with sarsen stones, buried beneath a mound of earth. This in turn was lined with sarsen stones that possibly acted as a kerb around the mound. This is one of a number of similar burial mounds or barrows found in the Medway area and the design has more in common with barrows found in Western Europe than those in the rest of the British Isles.*

- After viewing Little Kits Coty, return to the road and walk along it with care for 300 yards to reach a road junction.
- Bear right around the bend for a few yards until you reach the Pilgrims' Way going off on the right. Cross the road at this point, turn left for 10 yards, then turn right onto a footpath on the right (signed 'North Downs Way').
- Climb the tree-lined track for 200 yards to the top of the slope, to reach Kits Coty on your left.

**The imposing entrance to the Neolithic burial mounds of Kits Coty.**

*Kits Coty was a communal burial mound, built around 2200BC, and later than Little Kits Coty at the foot of the hill. Although this has been identified as a long barrow, it now appears more likely that it is the type of tomb known as a 'portal dolmen'. This is a small rectangular stone chamber, buried beneath a mound of earth, with the entrance marked by two huge upright stones capped by a sloping roofstone, which projects beyond the upright to form a sort of porch. As the mound subsides over the centuries, the roofstone collapses into the shape seen today.*

*By the time Kits Coty was built it had become the tradition to put burial mounds on high airy places. Whether this had religious significance or whether it was to give the mounds an additional use as a territorial marker, is unknown. Certainly by now communities were starting to become linked to specific geographic areas, and more permanent settlements with permanent territories were developing.*

*Those buried under the mound are more likely to have been people of religious importance, priests or shamans, than political leaders. The mound was named 'Kit's Coty' in the Middle Ages, meaning the house (or 'coty') of Kit, or Catigern, an Iron Age chieftain supposedly buried there. The mound is, however, far older than the Iron Age and there is no reason to believe it contains any such person.*

- Continue up the trackway, ignoring side turns. Eventually climb some steps with a fence on your left to reach a road.
- Turn left along the road for 200 yards, passing the entrance to 'Beechcroft', then use a footbridge to cross the A229.
- On the far side of the footbridge, keep ahead up the right-hand side of the A229 for 30 yards, then bear off right up a footpath, initially parallel to the road but soon bearing away from it.
- Turn right with the footpath to climb over a stile and up through trees to reach a lane.

*This lane follows the course of a Roman road, a spur that connected the Medway Valley with Watling Street, the main London–Dover road. Like all Roman roads, this would have had an all-weather surface which would have enabled travel to have continued regardless of the season of the year. The ancient Neolithic trackways along the foot of the Downs were reduced to quagmires in wet weather and effectively all communications ceased in the winter.*

- Turn left in lane and follow it for a third of a mile, to where it swings left at a '30mph' sign. The lane is now Mill Lane again.
- Retrace your outward journey for a quarter of a mile by keeping straight on to reach the Upper Bell Inn, then crossing the crossroad and keeping ahead to reach the car park.

WALK 3

# Oldbury Hill: Hill forts and trade routes in the Iron Age

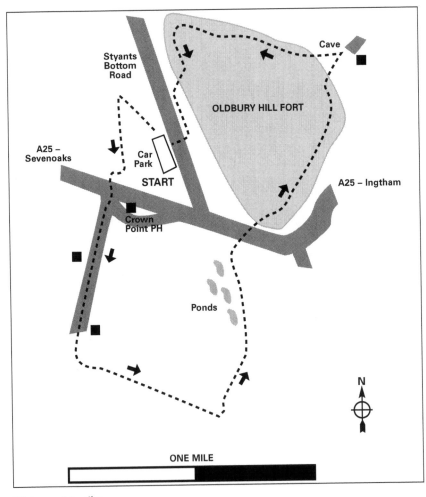

**Distance:** 4.5 miles

**Map:** OS sheet 188

**Start and Parking:** The walk commences from Oldbury Hill car park (NT), Styants Bottom Road, north off the A25 between Sevenoaks and Ightham (grid ref: 577558). If coming along the A25 from Sevenoaks, pass Crown Point car park on your right: immediately beyond it on the left is a bus stop pull-in. Styants Bottom Road is a narrow lane immediately at the end of the bus stop. If coming from Oldbury, pass Coach Road on your left and immediately look for a National Trust signpost, pointing to the car park down a lane to the right. The concealed car park entrance is 200 yards down the Styants Bottom lane on your left. An alternative starting point is the Crown Point lay-by on the A25 (grid ref: 577559).

**Refreshments:** Available at the Crown Point public house near the start of the walk.

### Historical Background

By the end of the Iron Age trade between the British tribes was extensive and trade goods came from as far afield as the Middle East and North Africa. A number of tribes had clans on both sides of the channel, and many tribes had strong cultural and trading links with their neighbours on the European mainland. Then, as now, most trade routes ran east–west from the harbours on the channel coast to the Thames Valley and beyond. Oldbury Hill stands upon one of the much rarer routes that ran north–south across the Weald, and it is the largest hillfort in Kent.

The first settlements upon Oldbury Hill were shelters established in caves by Palaeolithic hunters nearly 2,000 years ago, evidence of which can still be seen today. Towards the end of the Iron Age, around 100BC, a hillfort was constructed by local Wealdan tribes, both to provide shelter in times of trouble for their herds and people, and also to provide temporary shelter for traders. The fort was built on the top of Greensand Ridge, where two valleys running north–south through the steep-sided ridge provided a natural line of fortification. This fort occupied such an important strategic position that it was soon taken over by the Belgae, the foremost trading tribe of the time, which had a sturdy foothold in both southern Britain and northern Europe. The Belgae extended the site to cover 151 acres, and greatly improved its fortifications. Oldbury was soon of major importance to the Belgae. It was an extensive settlement in its own right as well as an important and strategically-placed trading post, and as such was defended fiercely but in vain against the advancing Roman legions in AD43.

### The Walk

This walk travels along the wooded Greensand Ridge, following part of the ancient Iron Age trade route into Oldbury Hill Fort, to visit the fort itself.

- From the Oldbury Hill car park, proceed to the far end, passing under the overhead exit barrier. Immediately turn sharp left onto a bridle path.
- After 100 yards, at a crossing bridlepath, turn left, soon climbing steeply up to the A25.
- Turn left to the main road and cross with care to the uphill corner of the Crown Point lay-by. The Crown Point Inn lies below you in the dip, and a stone-faced cottage faces you. (If parked at Crown Point, your starting point is the top of the lay-by.)
- Follow the broad drive to the left of the stone-faced cottage at the top of the lay-by. The drive, soon tarmacked, continues for 600 yards to the end, passing a house to your left.

- Continue in the same direction along a bridle path, leaving leftwards from behind the house.
- Climb on the path to a gate. Turn left into a cross track beyond the gate and proceed, with steep drops down to Stone Street soon emerging on your right.
- After 600 yards, at the point where the trees on your left drop away into a hollow, turn left steeply downhill on a path through the woods.

*You are now following the course of the old prehistoric road, which ran from the south coast near Pevensey to the Thames. It climbed from the Medway Valley around Tonbridge, crossed the ridge at the point you are now at, and then proceeded to the confluence of the Medway and the Thames, near present day Rochester. This journey, which forced the traveller to leave the open ridges and traverse the dark and forbidding forest, could easily have taken two days, especially if stock were being driven. However, overnight comfort and protection was near at hand, in the form of Oldbury Camp, a mile ahead down the path.*

- Continue ahead and down when joined by another track from the right, eventually passing a series of small pools to your left.

*Pools have existed beside the path since prehistoric times, and would have provided welcome watering holes for travellers and stock, just driven over the high ridge behind.*

- Look for a path to your right, leading off opposite the fourth pool, and follow this out to the A25. This path can be hard to find in the summer undergrowth, but if it is missed, do not worry; just follow the main path you are on until the A25 is reached.
- Turn right along the A25 and cross the road to a bus stop pull-in on the opposite side of the road. (The junction of the A25 and Coach Road is visible, 50 yards further along the main road, on the right.) Behind the bus stop is a National Trust sign board.

*You are now at the southern gateway of Oldbury Castle, with its ramparts, two and a half miles long, towering above you. Two thousand years ago these ramparts would have been bare earth, not wooded as today, and a strong wooden gate would have been present to bar progress if necessary. The gate was always the weakest part of a fort, and most forts would have had one or at most two gates. Oldbury had two. The gate itself would have been a movable wooden structure, often a pile of logs, inside intricate earth ramparts that defended it. These ramparts are clearly visible here at Oldbury's southern gate.*

- Facing the sign board, take the right-hand path, climbing above the A25 on your right, for 150 yards.
- Still climbing, turn left with the path. Fifty yards beyond the corner, turn right at a cross track through a barrier and up a few natural steps.
- Follow the broad track ahead along the lower ramparts.

*Today the view is obscured by trees, but 2,000 years ago the ramparts would have been clear, with views commanding the surrounding countryside. The banks would have been more precipitate than today and a strong wooden palisade would have faced downhill, giving further protection in times of trouble.*

- Ignore a waymarked track on the left, and keep straight on with drops to your right.
- Keep straight on at a cross track.
- After a further 150 yards, you come to a waymarked cross track with a steep path dropping through a cutting to your right. Ignore this downhill track, but take the track next to it, the rightmost of two straight on tracks.
- After 50 yards, bear right at a junction.
- Go down steps and through a cleft in the rock.

The ramparts of Coldbury Castle Hill Fort.

*At the bottom of the steps, look to the left behind a fallen tree, up a bank. The cave you see is one of several rock dwellings on the hill occupied by the Palaeolithic hunters who pre-dated the castle by many centuries. These dwellings were more than just a temporary overnight shelter, and were occupied for many weeks at a time during the hunting season. Formed by natural erosion within the sandstone, the floor would have been covered by rushes and skins to provide some measure of comfort.*

- After looking at the rock dwelling, continue down the path. Turn right around a garage, and up the bridleway to the side of the house.
- Go straight ahead up a steep and sunken track, passing back through the ramparts to a cross track, encountered earlier, at the top of the slope. Now go straight on along the bridleway.
- Continue along the bridleway, passing a National Trust board to your left and orchards through the trees to your right.

*You soon pass near the site of an ancient spring, which drains into a pool on your left. This spring provided drinking water for the fort in times of siege, and lay immediately beside the north–south road, along which you entered the fort and which continues towards present day Rochester.*

- After 600 yards you come to a junction of paths. Ignore those to left and right, and take the left-most of the three that go straight on.
- After 50 yards, turn sharp left with the path. You are now at the most spectacular part of the fortifications, walking between two sets of ramparts.

*Again, none of the woods which fill the vista would have existed. To your right, clear views would have commanded the surrounding countryside. To your left, within the inner rampart, would have been a vast open space, covering 150 acres. In times of peace, the hillfort would have been an administrative and commercial centre for the tribe, and would have had huts for the regular inhabitants, stockades and temporary accommodation for passing traders. The bulk of the tribe would have lived in outlying farms in the countryside beyond. There was a flourishing iron-working industry nearby, and the produce of the forges would have been traded here.*

*In times of war, the fort would have provided emergency shelter for the neighbourhood, and in the centre was plenty of open space to house the cattle of the surrounding farms. It is still just possible to make out the occasional outline of a hut circle or a grain pit amid the oak groves and chestnut coppices that now cover the site, and it is rewarding to wander through the middle of the old fort and let your imagination loose.*

- After 300 yards, turn right down some wooden steps. Keep straight ahead at the foot of the steps.

- Just before a lane is reached, turn left onto a cross track. Follow the track for 300 yards to join the lane opposite Oldbury Hill car park.
- If you started from Crown Point, cross the lane and immediately before the overhead barrier of the car park exit, turn up a bridlepath to the right. Now follow the first instructions of this walk to return to Crown Point.
- Sandwich experienced a renaissance in the early 16th century, when an influx of Flemish refugees brought weaving skills into the town, and also brought land reclamation skills that re-opened water channels and drained marshland, facilitating market gardening.

WALK 4

# Richborough and the Roman invasion of Britain

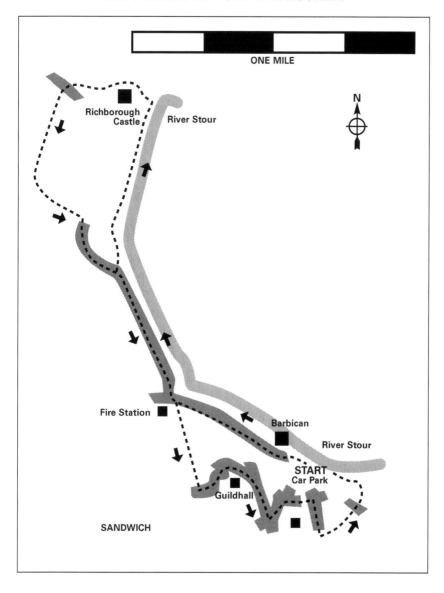

ONE MILE

Richborough Castle

River Stour

N

Fire Station

Barbican

River Stour

START
Car Park

Guildhall

SANDWICH

**Distance:** 4.5 miles
**Map:** OS sheet 179
**Start and Parking:** The walk commences from the old quay in Sandwich (grid ref: 334582). Sandwich is on the A256, seven miles south of Ramsgate and six miles north of Deal. There is ample pay-and-display car parking on the quay itself.
**Refreshments:** Public houses, shops and cafés in Sandwich.

### Historical Background

In AD43, 50,000 Roman troops landed at Richborough and swept up through Kent to conquer Britain for the Emperor Claudius. A fort was built at Richborough, soon to be replaced by a flourishing town, the main entry into Britain for the next two centuries. Deteriorating military conditions led to the town being demolished to make way for a strong fort around AD250. This was built to command the southern entrance of the Wantsum Channel, an area of mud flats and creeks separating the Isle of Thanet from the mainland. For 150 years Richborough was a vital link in the string of forts built to protect the Saxon shore. Although it continued to be used by the British even after the Romans abandoned Britain in AD410, Richborough gradually sank into disuse.

In its place the town of Sandwich developed a mile to the south. Sandwich was an important town in Saxon times, and in the Doomsday Book of 1086 it was ranked the fourth most important town in England, after London, Norwich and Ipswich. Its prominence increased still further with the arrival of the Normans. Sandwich was one of the original Cinque Ports (from the french 'cinq' or 'five'), who were granted lucrative trading advantages by the Crown in return for providing boats for use by the king in time of war or national emergency. The town flourished until the 14th century, when the silting up of the harbour led to a gradual decline in its trade.

### The Walk

**This walk goes around the historic old town of Sandwich, one of the best preserved historic towns in England, and across the fenlands of the Stour estuary to the mighty Richborough Castle.**

● From the Old Quay car park, with the river on your right, walk along the old quay towards the bridge. Do not cross the bridge, but pause at the end of it and look at the gatehouse, or 'barbican'.

*Initially Sandwich stood at the head of a small inlet, emptying into the Wantsum Channel. It was thus protected from the worst of the seas and had easy access across the channel, north and south along the English coast, and inland through rivers and creeks. It also had good road access up the Roman Watling Street, to Canterbury and beyond. Its name means 'town built on the sands', an eloquent statement of its original position.*

*The old quay was the harbour-front of Sandwich in its heyday. A huge fishing fleet operated out of Sandwich in the Middle Ages: the town paid a rent of 40,000 herring a year to Canterbury Cathedral in 1086. In addition, as one of the original five Cinque Ports, the merchant vessels trading from Sandwich were among the most prosperous in Britain. They traded for wines, silks, spices and other luxury goods across the whole of Europe with produce brought from all over the British Isles, either around the coast or down the road from Canterbury and London.*

*Sandwich's sheltered harbour, with ready access to the Continent and to London, was a favourite entry and exit point for travellers. A key character in the Kentish story, Thomas-à-Becket, left England into exile from Sandwich in 1163, and landed on this quay on his return seven years later.*

*Initially Sandwich had no town walls. The houses facing the harbour were stoutly built for defence, and this was reinforced by churches built initially as mini fortresses. The Barbican was not part of the original town defences. It was added in 1539, at the same time that Deal, Walmer and Sandown Castles were built, as part of the line of coastal defences built by Henry VIII to give protection against the French.*

● Turn left from the end of the bridge and pass through the Barbican gateway, and then turn right in front of the Admiral Owen public house, to go down Strand Street.
● Go down Strand Street, ignoring side turnings.

*Originally the river was much wider, with a bank or 'stronde' along its southern side. This 'stronde' or 'strand' became the main street in the town, with narrow gaps at intervals between the close packed houses to allow passage onto the only dry road leading inland. These gaps became the narrow side streets you see today.*

*Strand Street has the greatest collection of timber-framed buildings found anywhere in England. Some of the best examples are 'The Weavers', home to Flemish refugees from religious persecution who settled in Sandwich in the early 16th century (opposite Kings Yard) and 'The Pilgrims', two early 15th-century merchants houses (at the junction with Harnet Street).*

● Where Harnet Street joins from the left keep straight on, passing St Mary's Church.

*Prior to 1380 Sandwich had no town walls. Part of its defences were churches built as fortresses to provide sanctuaries as well as places of worship. The Church of St Mary the Virgin had such a dual purpose, and was severely damaged during French raids in 1217 and in 1457.*

*The church had a long and eventful history. It was originally given as a nunnery by Ethelbert King of Kent, who had married a Christian princess, Bertha, and was inclined towards the Christian religion. It was Ethelbert's ready conversion that so eased St Augustine's mission in AD697 (see walk 7). The nunnery site was used by the Normans to build a fortress church. This was damaged by an earthquake in 1578, undermining the foundations to the extent that the tower collapsed in the next century and the church was abandoned until very recently.*

● Follow Strand Street past the magnificent Manwood Court to reach Gallows field.

*Gallows Field was just outside the Canterbury Gate through the town walls, which were built in 1380. It was an execution site for felons and was used up until 1792, when two deserters from the army were hanged.*

- Turn right into Richborough Road, opposite the Kent Fire Brigade Station.
- Go up Richborough Road. Continue to follow the lane through fields and past isolated houses.
- Where the lane bends left, just before passing under the elevated road bridge of the A256 and by a level crossing sign, go right through a kissing gate beside a metal field gate.
- Keep straight on along a broad track, with the River Stour to the right, soon passing under the A256.
- Continue ahead, still with the river on your right and soon with a railway to your left.
- After two thirds of a mile cross a stile and over a sluice gate.
- At a T-junction, where the river bends sharply to the right, turn left and cross over the railway track.

*The walls of Richborough fort can now be seen ahead of you.*

- Carefully cross the railway track, and cross a stile on the other side of the railway. Do not cross a second stile immediately on your left, but instead turn right. Pass to the right of outbuildings and onto a track.
- Turn left with the track and climb a slope, with garden of a house on your left.

*Richborough was the foremost port in Roman Britain. The temporary fort built in AD43 to protect the beachhead of the Roman invasion was demolished as the rapid pacification of Kent made it redundant. Richborough grew into a major military and naval supply base, in the centre of which stood a huge triumphal arch, straddling the way from the port to Watling Street and the rest of Britain, a symbolic entrance into the new Roman province. Soon a port named Rutupiae grew up under the protection of the fort, with warehouses and merchants dwellings growing up around the harbour, and taverns, hostels, baths and an amphitheatre being added as the town flourished. Imports and exports flowed through Rutupiae, which became the gateway to Britain.*

*Rutupiae flourished as a commercial centre for 200 years. By the middle of the third century pirate activity was seriously interrupting trade, and raids from Gaul on to the coast were becoming common. Much of the town centre was demolished and rebuilt as a strong castle, to provide a secure base for dealing with these raiders. It was surrounded initially by a double and in places triple line of ditches and ramparts, with immense stone walls inside these. Richborough Castle commanded the southern end of the Wantsum channel, while Reculver commanded the northern (see walk 5).*

*The harbour and much of the surrounding town were lost beneath the sea, which covered the flat lands you have walked across from Sandwich. The remainder of the town was largely lost beneath the third-century fort, whose walls, ditches and ramparts you see before you. Inside these walls are to be found traces of the fort buildings, and the foundations of the immense arch that dominated the town.*

Richborough Castle, the gateway to the
Roman province of Britannia.

Richborough Castle is open from 1 April to 30 September, 10am–6pm. There is an
admission charge, but it is free to members of English Heritage.

- Continue along the track, following it as it bends left along the castle walls and then
  right towards houses ahead.

*The course of the old Wantsum Channel can be seen as the flat land to the right. Behind the
power station seen in the distance is Ebbsfleet, where St Augustine landed in AD597 on his
mission to convert Britain back to Christianity (see walk 7).*

- Join a flinty track and keep straight on, passing a row of houses on your right, to
  reach a lane.
- Cross the lane and enter a field opposite. Follow the footpath down the right-hand
  side of the field, keeping the field boundary on your right.
- Pass into a second field and keep straight on, still with the field boundary on the
  right.
- At the bottom of the field enter the next field and bear quarter left across the next
  field, aiming for a marker post 100 yards away in the middle of the field.
- At the marker post turn left and walk with a drainage ditch on your right.
- Cross a stile by a gate and keep straight on down an enclosed path. In 50 yards ignore
  a turning to the right and then very shortly ignore one to the left.
- Keep straight on along the top of a bank. Do not descend but keep ahead into a field.

- Keep straight on across the field, aiming at a gate to the right of some brick and concrete pillars seen ahead.
- Cross a stile by the gate and into a lane. Turn right along the lane and follow it as it winds through fens, until in a quarter of a mile it crosses the railway and then passes under a road bridge.
- This is Richborough Road again. Follow it back to Gallows Field. On reaching the main road again, cross the road and turn left in front of the fire station.
- After 50 yards turn right down The Butts.

*Norman feudalism was based on the concept that everyone, from the richest lord to the smallest farmer, held land in exchange for providing military service. In reality, it was the nobility who provided the professional soldiers, and their retainers were conscripted when required, with little or no training in the arts of war.*

*This altered in the middle of the 14th century, under the demands of the Hundred Years War. England had developed a weapon which was to dominate the battlefields of Europe for 200 years, namely the longbow. In skilled hands this weapon could drive a metal tipped arrow through the thickest armour at a range of 250 yards. To ensure this skill existed a form of military service was introduced: every commoner was required on pain of fines to practice with the longbow for two hours every week, after the Sunday church service was finished. An area was set aside for this practice, usually waste ground abutting the town walls, and named after the straw targets used, known as 'butts'.*

- Stay on the concrete pavement to the right of the drive and walk along the old town wall.

*The town walls in Sandwich were built comparatively late, in 1380. The advent of gunpowder had rendered the previous defences – fortified churches and strong houses – useless, and so the town was encircled with walls, stone built on the northern, seaward side, and here on the west and south, an earth embankment topped with a wooden palisade and fronted by a deep ditch.*

*The influx of Protestant refugees fleeing from religious persecution in Flanders during the late 15th century brought with it not only weaving skills but also skills in hydrodynamics. The marshes outside the town were drained, land reclaimed for arable use, and a clean water supply provided to meet the town's needs.*

- On reaching a road turn left and follow the road, passing St Thomas' Hospital on your left.

*St Thomas' Hospital is a comparatively new building, but there has been a hospital on this site since 1392. This was not a 'hospital' in todays meaning of the word, but rather a 'hospice', providing shelter for the poor rather than medical care. This is one of three founded in Sandwich by wealthy benefactors in the 13th and 14th century, and is named after Thomas Becket.*

- At a mini roundabout, turn right. 50 yards later turn left and walk ahead to a T-junction in front of the New Inn. Turn right here to reach the square in front of the Guildhall in 10 yards.

*The Guildhall was the central council chamber of mediaeval Sandwich, and reflects in its name that local government was the domain of the merchants' guilds. It served as a courtroom as well as a council chamber, and assizes were held here until 1951. The present building dates from 1579 and contains largely unaltered architectural features from the Elizabethan and Stuart periods.*

**Guided tours are available Tuesday–Thursday, 11.30am and 2.30pm, and Fridays 11.30am, in season.**

- Pass in front of the Guildhall and along New Street. Almost immediately turn left down Austins Lane and then turn right into King Street.

*St Peter's Church is another of the Norman fortress churches of Sandwich. Like St Mary's, it was badly damaged in the French raid of 1217.*

- At a road junction at the Post Office continue ahead to reach a cross roads. Here turn sharp left down The Chain.
- In 60 yards turn right and keep ahead to St Clements.

*St Clement's has a superb Norman tower chancel and central nave. The nave aisles were added in the 15th century. Unlike St Mary's and St Peter's, this church escaped the ravages of French raids, being in the corner of the town furthest from the sea. Since 1948 it has been the Parish Church of Sandwich.*

- Pass through the churchyard, with the church on your right. Leave the churchyard and turn right up a no through road, with the rear of the church on your right.
- Keep ahead up this road to reach the town walls again.
- Turn left on to a tarmacked path along the town wall.

*The ditch and rampart that formed the landward side of the town walls can clearly be seen here. The rampart you are walking along would have been topped with a wooden palisade.*

- Cross a road and continue along the wall, now fenced on your right and called The Bulwark.
- Turn left with the wall and follow footpath back to the quay and the car park.

WALK 5

# Reculver: Roman forts and Saxon churches

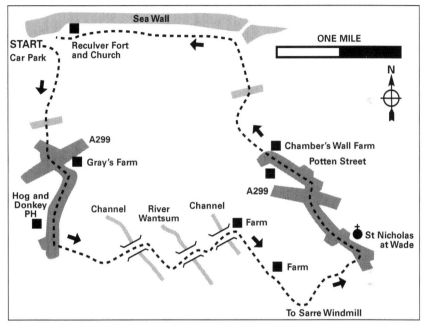

**Distance:** 10 miles

**Map:** OS sheet 179

**Start and parking:** The walk commences from the car park of Reculver Country Park (grid ref: 225693), at the end of a minor road, clearly signposted from the A299 Thanet Way.

**Refreshments:** Pubs and cafés around Reculver Country Park: Hog and Donkey pub two miles along the route: pubs and shop at St Nicholas at Wade.

### Historical Background

In Roman and Saxon times, the coastline in this part of Kent was very different from today. Thanet was still an island, separated from the mainland by a sea channel, called the Wantsum Channel, which connected the Thames estuary and the English Channel. This was a desolate landscape of tidal marshes and mud flats, between one and three miles wide, with a winding stretch of navigable water running through it. The Romans built two forts to command this channel, Richborough at the southern end (see walk 4)

41

and Reculver at the northern end. These were part of a series of forts constructed to control the estuaries and navigable waterways of Britain's south-eastern coastline, known as the Saxon Coast.

The fort at Reculver was originally nearly a mile from the sea (the present church stands almost in the middle of the old fort), but during the intervening centuries the coastline has encroached and over half the fort is now submerged. At the same time the Wantsum Channel has silted up, and gradually dried out, and the area has gradually been reclaimed as agricultural land. The Romans built Reculver around AD200 and garrisoned it until Roman authority collapsed towards the end of the fourth century, after which the fort fell into disuse.

In AD669 Egbert, King of Kent, gave the land to Christian missionaries and by AD692 there was an important monastery on the site. The church survived the troubled eighth and ninth centuries with very little damage. Although the monastery had ceased to exist by the 10th century, the church remained as the parish church of the area until the end of the 18th century, by which time the sea had encroached so far that the inhabitants of the parish moved to drier ground.

The church was partially dismantled to provide building material for a new parish church at Hillborough and the rest left to the mercy of the sea, but in 1809 Trinity House bought the remains, primarily the twin towers, as a navigation aid for vessels entering the Thames estuary.

### The Walk
**This walk follows part of the old Saxon shoreline and crosses the now reclaimed Wantsum Channel, an area of sea in Roman times. It returns along the coast to visit the remains of Roman and Saxon Reculver.**

- Leave the entrance to Reculver Country Park car park and, facing the King Ethelbert Hotel, turn right down the road. After 100 yards, behind a pillar box and telephone kiosk and just before the café, turn left up a no through road signposted to 'Reculver Caravan Site'.
- Where the concrete drive turns into the entrance to Reculver Caravan site, continue straight on down an enclosed track between parts of the caravan park.
- After 200 yards and just before a gate, where the track emerges into open fields, turn right past a power line and follow the path alongside a water channel.
- Continue straight on across the top of a field. Carry straight on, with a channel on your right, along the side of a field to a footbridge.
- Cross the footbridge and continue on alongside the channel to reach a gate on to a drive.
- Pass through the gate, turn right along the drive for 10 yards, then turn left along a concrete drive to pass under the railway. Follow the concrete drive gently uphill for 400 yards to reach a lane.
- At the lane, turn left for 10 yards to reach a T-junction, then turn right down the road signposted 'Marshside'.

- Follow the road for 250 yards as it swings left and then crosses the A299 Thanet Way by a road bridge, with the Roman Galley Hotel to your left.
- At a T-Junction on the far side of the road bridge, turn left. Follow this quiet lane as it swings right and downhill through Grays Farm, and then through Little Greys. Continue along the lane once it has levelled out, now with a water channel along the left side, passing the remote Hog and Donkey public house on your right.

*You are now walking along what in Roman times was the shoreline. To your right the land slopes gently upwards; to your left is what used to be the Wantsum Channel, a flat expanse of water, reeds and mud flats stretching over a mile before reaching the opposite shore, just discernible as a slight rise at what is now St Nicholas at Wade.*

- Four hundred yards past the Hog and Donkey, where a small lane branches off to the right, turn left across a bridge over the channel and through a field gate onto a bridle path.
- Continue along the bridle path as it winds through fields. After 800 yards, fork left at a junction.
- Continue for another half mile along the bridle path as it winds through fields, with bushes and trees along the path edges for many sections, to reach a gate.
- Pass through the gate, cross a dyke by a tractor bridge, and turn right onto a permissive path along the top of the dyke.
- Continue along the dyke, with the channel to your right, for 600 yards, passing two wooden footbridges across the channel. 20 yards after passing the second footbridge, turn left onto an adjoining bridle path.
- Follow the bridle path between fields, with intermittent hedges and spinneys on your left, maintaining generally the same direction, to reach a concrete bridge across a water channel.

*You are now crossing the River Wantsum. Until now all the fenland you have crossed since leaving the lane by the Hog and Donkey was tidally submerged in Roman and Saxon times. You are now crossing the navigable channel that ran through the marshes and mudflats of the Wantsum Channel.*

- Cross the bridge and follow the winding metalled drive to cross a second bridge.

*You have now reached what in Saxon times was the far shore of the Wantsum Channel.*

- Cross this second bridge and follow the drive, passing a farm on your left. As the drive swings leftwards, ignore bridges on your right, but a few yards further on, opposite a cottage, turn right onto a bridle path.
- Follow the bridle path, with hedges on the right and soon with a channel on right. After 400 yards, ignore a bridge on your right and continue straight on, with the channel on your right. Where the path leaves the channel, continue straight ahead along a clear path across a field, towards farm buildings.

- Just before farm buildings, where the main bridle path turns left, keep straight on along a lesser track. After 20 yards, where this track turns left into the farmyard, go straight on through a gate onto a grassy track. Follow this track for a few yards as it bends to the left.
- Although the right of way now goes into the corner of the yard ahead, follow the permissive diversion by aiming half-right through the small caravan parking area in front of you. Pass between caravans and leave through a narrow gate in the middle of the hedge in front.
- Continue straight on in the same direction, along a clear bridle path in front of you. Follow the bridle path, soon with a hedge on your right, as it bends around field boundaries, for 600 yards.
- Where a tarmacked path joins from the left, turn left onto a tarmacked path and follow it slightly uphill across a field.

*If you wish to visit Sarre Windmill, a working windmill and animal farm open to the public, continue straight on along the bridle path at this point.*

**Sarre Windmill is open daily 10am–5pm.**

- Follow the path, initially tarmacked, for 800 yards across fields, ignoring a bridle path leading off to the right. On the outskirts of St Nicholas at Wade the path reaches a turning circle at the end of a cul-de-sac, with a strategically positioned bench.

*Sitting on the bench you are afforded fine views over the Wantsum Channel and of Sarre Windmill. Although the Wantsum Channel was navigable from north to south, there were also fords which crossed the marshes from the Kentish mainland to the Isle of Thanet. One such ford was just in front of you, running left to right, from where Sarre Windmill now stands to Upstreet on the Kentish side of the channel.*

- Follow the tarmacked path around the left-hand boundary of a field, and then across a second field to enter a recreation field.
- Continue straight on along the right-hand edge of the recreation field. The path soon becomes enclosed, and shortly passes through a gate to reach a road.
- Turn left for 20 yards up the road to reach a T-junction.
- Turn left at the T-junction and proceed along the main street of St Nicholas at Wade, passing between two public houses and shortly passing the church on your right.

*The church of St Nicholas is 13th century with an early 14th-century tower. Inside are arches in the chancel dating from around AD1200 and an interesting wooden staircase leading to a lobby above the porch.*

- One hundred yards past the church, at a junction of roads, fork right down Court Road.
- Continue along the road for half a mile, ignoring turns to left and right.

- The road crosses the A299 Thanet Way via a road bridge, from the top of which there are fine views.

*The twin towers of Reculver can just be seen on the skyline, above the sea wall that now demarks the limit of the reclaimed fenlands.*

- Cross the A299 and follow the road to a T-junction, where you turn left, signposted 'Potten Street'.
- In 200 yards, where the road swings right at Potten Street, continue straight on. Follow the lane for a further 400 yards to pass through Chambers Wall Farm.
- Immediately after passing the farm, where the lane swings left, turn right across a small bridge onto a concrete track.
- Follow the concrete track for half a mile. Where the concrete ends, bear right, with a hedge on your right, soon to join a track along the top of a dyke, with the water channel to your left.
- Continue along the dyke for 600 yards to cross the railway.
- On the far side of the railway track, turn right with the track to the top of the dyke, then immediately cross the dyke and descend leftwards to pick up the continuation of the track you have been following. Turn right onto the track and go along the top of the dyke, with a water channel on your left.
- After 600 yards the track reaches a metalled path along the top of a sea wall. Turn left along this path, with drained marshes on your left and the recently reclaimed lagoon on your right.
- After 200 yards the path reaches the coast.

*Reculver Towers can be seen in front of you. Trinity House, the body responsible for ensuring safe navigation around Britain's coasts, bought the towers in 1809 to save them from demolition, on the grounds that they provided a distinctive landmark for shipping entering the Thames estuary. Their domination of the landscape can clearly be seen for the remainder of this walk.*

- Follow the sea wall for one and a half miles, with Reculver Towers getting ever closer to you.

*The beach on your right was used during World War Two as a testing ground for many weapons, among the most well known of which was the 'Bouncing Bomb', designed by Barnes Wallis and used in the famous Dambusters' raid. A complete prototype bomb was dug up from this beach in the summer of 1997, where it had lain since being tested over 50 years earlier.*

*If you look to your left as you walk along the sea wall you will be able to clearly distinguish both shores of the old Wantsum Channel.*

- The path eventually reaches Reculver.

A Saxon church stands behind the Roman fort of Reculver.

*You are now passing through what used to be the Roman port. The sea was a mile to your right and the fort was on the headland ahead of you, which provided a sheltered anchorage.*

● Turn left along the foot of the old Roman fort.

*On your right is a surviving section of the Roman fort wall. Clearly visible are the layers of flint and mortar alternated to provide the wall with extra strength.*

● At a T-junction, turn right through the east gate of Reculver fort.

*The Roman fort at Reculver was nearly 600 square feet, surrounded by walls 15 feet high and 10 feet thick. It was built upon a natural rise of land, and the rubbish accumulated during two centuries of occupation raised the level of the fort still more. It had a garrison of around 1,000 men, and it contained all the facilities necessary for their comfort, including barracks, bath-house and a temple. Over the intervening centuries the sea has advanced by a mile, and swept away the north and west walls of the fort. A pathway leading from the east gate still follows the course of the surviving east and south walls. Nothing remains to be seen of the buildings inside the fort.*

● Follow the path, passing the church on your right.

*Much of the church has been demolished, either eroded by the sea or pulled down for building materials. The oldest part of the church is the nave, built in AD669. The bottoms of these Saxon walls still survive. The church was small, with an aisle-less nave and rounded chancel, a design typical of early churches in Kent. The original walls and the eighth-century extension are marked out on the ground.*

*The church was remodelled in the 12th century. The twin towers were added, with a main west entrance between them. They were originally topped with wooden spires, but these blew down in 1818. Although the stairs up to the third storey of these towers survive, they are no longer open to the public.*

**Both the church and the fort are open to the public at any reasonable time.**

● Follow the path to emerge above the car park.

*The ruins of Herne Bay Pier can be seen out to sea, in front of you and to your right. The pier was destroyed by storms in the early 1980s, but the pier head survived and still stands, now isolated half a mile out to sea.*

WALK 6

# The Darenth Valley:
# 2,000 years of commuters

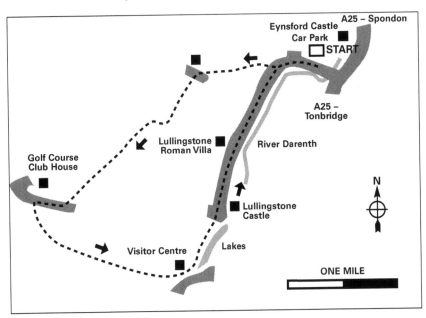

**Distance:** 5.5 miles

**Map:** OS sheet 177

**Start and Parking:** The walk commences in Eynsford village (grid ref: 539656). From the A225 from London, turn right across a hump-backed bridge in the village centre, in the direction of Lullingstone Villa and Castle. Park in the public car park behind the Plough Inn, Lynsford.

**Refreshments:** Pubs, tearoom and a shop in Eynsford: Clubroom of Lullingstone Golf Course opens to the public: soft drinks and snacks at Lullingstone Castle Visitors' Centre.

### Historical Background

Today the charming Darenth Valley, especially its northern end around Eynsford, Shoreham and Otford, is often thought of as being a dormitory for London commuters. Although there is still a considerable amount of local employment in the area, it is true that a considerable percentage of the working population take advantage of the easy access into London to work in the city while living in a green and pleasant valley.

What is less frequently realised is that this area has in a very real sense been a home for London 'commuters' throughout the ages. True, prior to the Industrial Revolution and the arrival of the railway in the middle of the last century, the bulk of the population worked where they lived. But for wealthy courtiers, civil servants and merchants, whose public life revolved around the capital, the Darenth Valley has provided a pleasant and sheltered place to live within easy distance of London for 2,000 years. A Roman civil servant working in Londinium bought a farm at Lullingstone and converted it into a magnificent villa; a Norman baron built a castle as his home at Eynsford, conveniently close to the capital; a Tudor courtier built a mock castle at Lullingstone and installed a tiltyard for the entertainment of his monarch and his peers.

### The Walk
**This walk goes through the lovely countryside of the upper Darenth Valley, passing some splendid examples of Roman, Norman and Tudor architecture. It follows the river to return under one of the most spectacular 19th-century railway viaducts in south-east England.**

- Leave the car park behind the Plough Inn and turn right along the lane, walking upstream alongside the Darenth, away from the village centre.
- Continue through the village, past Home Farm on the left and ignoring a right-hand turn to Crockenfield.
- Houses finally fade away to an open valley. Look for the last house on the right, Meadow View. Fifty yards past Meadow View turn into a field at a footpath sign beside a gate on the right.
- Proceed diagonally across the field, ascending towards the top of the railway viaduct which can be glimpsed through the trees to your left.

*The arrival of the railway in the 1840s brought the Darenth Valley within commuting distance of London as never before. Eynsford, Shoreham and Otford all expanded from being essentially agricultural communities to providing homes for the more affluent workers in the city. The viaduct to your left is a splendid example of Victorian civil engineering and will be seen to its full later in the walk.*

- At the top of the field, cross the railway line with great care and follow the clear path through the next field to a stile leading onto a drive.
- Cross the drive and follow the path through the third field, making for the bottom corner of a fourth field. Fine views over the Darenth Valley open up to your left.
- Enter the fourth field and continue your general line of advance, along the bottom of the field. The grey roof of the building now housing Lullingstone Villa can just be glimpsed in the trees at the bottom of the slope.
- Cross a stile and turn right into an enclosed path. Proceed up hill for 100 yards, and then turn left into an open field.

● Continue straight ahead along a clearly defined path which follows the top of the Greensand Ridge. This path marks the western boundary of the Tudor deerpark that adjoined Lullingstone Castle. There are fine views down into the Darenth Valley to your left, looking across the old deerpark.

*Deer still roamed this park until the end of the last century, and oaks survive which were planted in Tudor times. Until the Middle Ages deer had freely grazed the woodland of England, and were the sole property of the king under the Laws of the Forest. By the end of the 15th century the forests had shrunk under encroachment by agriculture and the heavy demand for wood to provide charcoal. Increasingly the greater landowners would enclose large swathes of land and stock them with their own deer herds, especially bred and managed to provide hunting for the landowner and his guests. Continuing deforestation meant that soon deerparks were the only habitat for these once free-roaming animals.*

● Follow the path down into a dip, with a golf course to your left, and up the other side. Bear slightly left to enter the woods ahead.
● Climb up through the woods by gentle wooden steps. In the right season a mass of bluebells are to be seen. After 200 yards emerge onto the side of the golf course.
● Proceed straight ahead, following the somewhat indistinct path along the right-hand edge of the golf course.
● At the end of the golf course, ignore the broad path directly ahead and bear slightly left to enter the woods.
● Wind through the open woodland, full of bluebells in May. The path often divides and reunites, but continue your line of advance, with the open golf course visible through the trees to your left.
● Join a broader track, and continue in the same general direction, still with the golf course to your left. Ignore cross tracks and continue forward.
● Eventually your path reaches a horse barrier. Pass through into a broad track and turn left.
● Cross between two fairways and keep straight ahead into the woods.
● Proceed through open woods, ignoring a cross track and continuing until you reach a tarmacked horse ride at the end of the woods. Turn right onto the tarmacked path, but look at the fine view down the valley to your left, once all deerpark but now a golf course.

*This shows an interesting change in land use. Once the preserve of the local landowner, for he and his friends to go hunting for recreation, the land is now open for recreation to the general public.*

● After 250 yards, turn left at public footpath sign (FP 206). (The clubhouse of Lullingstone Golf course is clearly visible to your right, and is open to the public for refreshments, reached by following the tarmacked path around.)
● Follow the footpath away from the golf course and down into woods. At the bottom of the slope, carefully cross the fairway and follow the broad path ahead up into the open woods on the other side of the valley.

- At a cross track, continue straight on, ignoring all turns to right and left.
- Emerge from the woods at the top of a dry valley falling away to your left. Continue straight on uphill, with fence and trees to your right.
- Re-enter the woods, and follow a broad track straight ahead, eventually passing through a horse barrier, to footpath signposts. Here go straight on (signed to 'Visitors' Centre').
- After 100 yards, take the right-hand fork, and follow the path downhill. You shortly emerge at the top of a wide meadow, with fine views down into the Darenth Valley, and with the Lullingstone Visitors' Centre clearly visible at the foot of the slope.
- Continue down the slope to the Visitors' Centre (refreshments available).
- Pass to the right of the Centre, to a stone bridge across the river. Do not cross the bridge, but just before it turn left onto a footpath along the riverbank.
- Follow this pleasantly shaded footpath along the river, with the old deerpark to your left, soon to reach a man-made weir and lake.

*This lake was constructed in Tudor times to provide fish for Lullingstone Castle and was used in Stuart times by the owners, the Hart family, for recreational fishing. The lake also provided water for a silkworm factory, run by the Hart family and their successors the Dyke family for many years.*

- Pass through the car park of Lullingstone Castle, to a tarmacked drive. Here turn left, in front of the castle.

*Although there has been a manor of Lullingstone since Domesday times, the current manor house dates from the reign of Henry VII, when it was built by Sir John Peche. A prominent courtier, Sir John took a leading part in the Royal Jousts of 1494, at which he won the prize, a golden ring with an inset diamond, which was presented to him by the king's younger daughter Margaret. A favourite of the king, Sir John became Sheriff of Kent in 1495, arresting the pretender Perkin Warbeck and being knighted for his part in the Battle of Blackheath in 1497. Sir John also went on to become a close companion of Henry VIII, becoming Lord Deputy of Calais and accompanying the King to his famous meeting with King Louis of France at the Field of the Cloth of Gold in 1520. As a prominent courtier, Sir John required a country retreat close to the court, which was located only a day's ride away at Greenwich, and which would be suitable for entertaining monarchy.*

*The splendid gatehouse was built in 1497, one of the earliest brick gatehouses in England and an imposing statement of the owner's pre-eminence. Sir John's coat-of-arms is emblazoned above the gates. To the west of this was a full-sized tiltyard, to cater for the passion for jousting which Sir John shared with Henry VIII. The surrounding park was enclosed and stocked with deer, again to cater for the monarch's passion for hunting. The ability to entertain the king close to his capital was part of the popularity of Lullingstone, and stood Sir John in good favour.*

*Upon Sir John's death the manor passed to his nephew Sir Percyvall Hart, who held court offices under Henry VIII, Edward VI, Mary and Elizabeth until his death in 1580. The Hart*

The Tudor gateway of Lullingstone Castle.

*family continued in the service of the Crown throughout the Stuart era, until the death of the last male Hart, also called Percival, in 1738. This Percival was a good friend of Queen Anne, another frequent royal visitor to Lullingstone. It was he who built the Queen Anne façade onto the castle and also made additions to the Tudor interior of the building. The adjoining Church of St Bodolph, open occasionally to the public, contains memorials to 600 years of the Peche, Hart and succeeding Dyke families.*

**Lullingstone Castle is open to the public weekends and bank holidays, April to September. The garden and church are open Wednesday–Friday afternoons, April to September. There is an admission charge.**

● Walk for half a mile along this drive to Lullingstone Roman Villa.

*At the time of the Roman Conquest in AD43 there was an Iron Age farmstead on the present site. About AD80 it was replaced by a small villa built by the first Romanised Britons in the area, a farming family who gradually extended the villa over the next 40 years and who remained in occupation for over a century. Just behind the villa was a small circular temple, devoted to the worship of the local woodland deity.*

*With Watling Street, the main Roman road from the coast to London passing only 20 miles to the north, the Darenth Valley became a desirable residence for government officials looking for a country retreat. Around AD180 a new owner took over the villa, not a British farmer but possibly a wealthy Roman of Mediterranean origin. This owner is believed to have been a civil servant, whose work often took him into Londinium for long periods of time, but who chose to live in the countryside rather than in the bustle of the city. The simple villa was now converted into a luxury residence: the thatch roof was replaced by one of red tiles, a bathing suite was added to the south end, the northern wing was extended and extensive redecoration in the Mediterranean style was undertaken.*

*The villa was suddenly abandoned around AD200, possibly as a result of the political unrest prevalent in Britain at that time, and remained unoccupied for most of the next century. About AD280 it was reoccupied, this time by wealthy Romano-Britons, who used the villa as a base for an extensive farm and built a temple mausoleum behind the house. It was these owners who laid the striking mosaics still to be seen in the dining room and reception room and among the best to be found in Britain today. Around AD390 the owners of the villa converted to Christianity, and built a chapel in the villa.*

*The villa was finally abandoned around AD420, and over the years the gradual movement of soil down the hillside buried and thus preserved the walls and floors.*

**Lullingstone Villa is open daily from 1 April to 30 September 10am–6pm and October to March 10am–4pm. There is an admission charge, but it is free to English Heritage members.**

● Passing the villa on your left, proceed down the quiet country lane, with the Darenth away to your left. After half a mile, the magnificent railway viaduct comes into view.

**Wonderfully preserved mosaic floor in the roman villa at Lullingstone.**

*Built of red brick in 1847 to carry the main Swanley to Sevenoaks line across the Darenth Valley, the construction of the viaduct played a major part in opening the valley to commuters. It was necessary for the line, which came from the North East, to cross from the western side of the valley in order to continue its southern course on the eastern side of the valley, where it avoided the privately-owned land of the large estates of the Darenth Valley.*

- Pass under the viaduct and continue along the lane. In quarter of a mile, pass Meadow View on your left, and follow your outward path back to the car park.
- It is worth detouring to see Eynsford Castle, a quarter of a mile's pleasant walk away. Pass in front of the Plough and cross the Darenth by the old hump-backed bridge, with the ford to your right. At the main road turn left. The Norman church opposite stands in a quiet country churchyard.
- Walk down the main road of Eynsford, still with reminders of its Tudor origin visible in such buildings as the Elizabeth Villas to your right.
- Turn left down what could be taken as a private driveway. Follow the drive around to the right to emerge at the ruins of Eynsford Castle.

*Eynsford Castle was originally built by William De Eynsford in 1090. De Eynsford was a Norman, who had come to England after the conquest. William the Conqueror had given the biggest estates in the more politically sensitive areas to the barons who had accompanied him to England, as a reward but also so that they could subdue the country. De Eynsford came to England somewhat after the conquest, and was more of a courtier than a military baron. He thus was content to be given a smaller estate which was nevertheless in good agricultural land and conveniently close to the court in London. Consequently, Eynsford Castle was never built for any real military purpose, but was instead a fortified home. Nevertheless, it is one of the finest examples of a 'pre re-keep' castle in England, the original style of Norman castles.*

*The castle is built upon an artificial mound of earth called a motte, and surrounded by a moat and a D-shaped flint curtain wall, which was 30 feet high but was never crenellated. This is a sure sign that it was never expected to be used for any serious fighting, but rather to protect the owner's property from casual banditry. There is no sign that the bridge over the moat could ever be raised. Entry to the castle was via a magnificent fortified gatehouse, which was roofed with tiles taken from Lullingstone Villa. Eynsford Castle never had a keep, but within the defensive curtain wall there was originally a wooden tower built above a well, which was eventually replaced by a stone two-storey manor house, of domestic rather than military design.*

*In the reign of Henry II, a later De Eynsford was ex-communicated by Archbishop Thomas Becket for taking certain feudal financial benefits from a local priest, which Becket considered an attack on the church. It was this sturdy defence of the privileges of the church against any encroachment by the secular powers that led to Becket's murder in 1170. After the murder it is claimed that De Eynsford was so overcome by remorse that he vowed never to live in his castle again. The castle was gutted by fire in 1261 and abandoned.*

**Eynsford Castle is open March to October, weekdays 9.30am–5.30pm, Sundays 2–5.30pm and November to February, weekdays 9.30am–4.00pm, Sundays 2–4pm. Entrance is free.**

WALK 7

# Canterbury and the return of Christianity to Britain

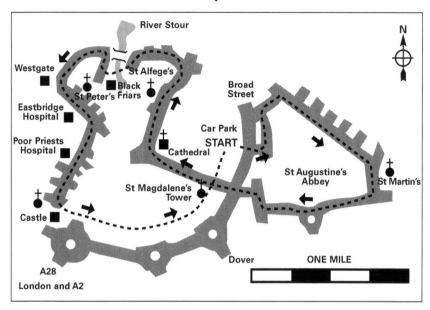

**Distance:** 3.5 miles

**Map:** OS sheet 179

**Start and Parking:** The walk starts at the Broad Street pay-and-display car park in Canterbury (grid ref: 153578). Broad Street is part of the inner ring road that circles the outside of Canterbury's mediaeval walls. It is the eastern sector midway between where the A2050 and the A28 join the ring road. The car park is against the town walls. There are several other car parks in Canterbury, but little street parking.

**Refreshments:** Public houses, shops, cafés and tearooms in Canterbury.

### Historical Background

There has been a settlement at Canterbury since at least 300BC. It stands at a place where a ford over the River Stour allowed an easy crossing for the important trade route from the coast to the Thames valley, and where the river valley provided an easy route southwards through the North Downs. The Romans defeated the local Britons and built a camp that eventually grew into the city of Durovernum. After the Romans left, Canterbury emerged as the capital of the kingdom of Kent: its name means 'stronghold of the people of Kent'.

Canterbury is closely linked with the story of the re-emergence of Christianity in England. In AD597 Augustine landed near Richborough and journeyed to Canterbury, where he was aided by Queen Bertha, herself a Christian, in converting her husband King Ethelbert, and through him his subjects. An abbey and a cathedral were established and, although often in rivalry, helped the newly-returned religion to flourish.

With the Norman invasion the position of Canterbury as both a commercial and a religious centre was consolidated. The Normans gave the church a great deal of secular power, leading to a conflict which culminated in the murder of Archbishop Thomas Becket in his own cathedral at Canterbury. This event immediately made Canterbury into one of the leading places of pilgrimage in Europe, requiring the development of a massive infrastructure to accommodate pilgrims, and greatly increasing the town's wealth and prosperity. Additionally, Canterbury became a centre of healing, attracting Dominican and Franciscan monks to settle in the town and build several hospitals.

The secular power of the church in Canterbury declined finally during Henry VIII's reign. The abbey was dissolved in 1538, Becket declared a traitor and his shrine looted, and the priory was dissolved in 1540. Cathedral buildings and wealth were secularised. The following century the cathedral was damaged by puritan extremists during the Civil War. Although Canterbury shared in the prosperity created by the wool trade in Tudor times, it never returned to its former pre-eminence.

**The Walk**
**This walk is entirely within the urban confines of old Canterbury, and its route follows the growth of Christianity in the city as well as passing sites that reflect its commercial and political power.**

- Walk down the Broad Street car park, with the town wall on your right, until you reach a postern gate in the wall (the Quentin Gate). With your back to the postern, leave the car park and cross the ring road at the pedestrian lights. Go straight on up Lady Woottons Green, with its hedge-lined flower garden in the centre.
- At the top of Lady Woottons Green, turn left in front of the gate of Christchurch College and follow the road past modern bungalows.
- At a T-junction, turn right into Havelock Street.
- After 150 yards, turn right along North Holmes Road. Keep ahead, keeping the ragstone wall of Christchurch College on your right. Keep straight on when the wall becomes brick, soon passing the houses of St Martins Terrace on your right.
- At the end of the terrace keep straight on, now with the railings of a churchyard on your left, to reach the entrance to St Martin's Church.

*St Martin's is England's oldest parish church. In AD562 Ethelbert, King of Kent, married Bertha of France, a Christian, who persuaded her new husband to build a church for her chaplain, Bishop Liudhard, in his capital Canterbury. This he duly did, and St Martin's Church was constructed sometime before AD570. As such, it pre-dated St Augustine's arrival*

Canterbury Cathedral, where Thomas Becket was
murdered in 1170.

*in Britain on his mission of conversion by over 25 years. The church was built in part of red Roman brick, still visible in places, has blocked-up Saxon windows and a fine pre-Norman fort.*

- Leave St Martin's via the lychgate and go straight ahead down the road, to meet the main road in 150 yards.
- Turn right along the main road for 300 yards, passing the entrance to Canterbury Prison, to reach St Augustine's Abbey.

*St Augustine landed in Kent in AD597, at Ebbsfleet near Richborough (see walk 4). He had been sent by Pope Gregory to convert the Britons back into Christianity, the religion they had followed in the last century of the Roman Empire. He was welcomed by King Ethelbert, already sympathetic to Christianity, and founded the abbey here at Ethelbert's capital in AD598, to house the monks who had accompanied him to England. Augustine called it the Abbey of St Peter and St Paul, and it was consecrated in AD613; later it became known as St Augustine's Abbey. Ethelbert, his Queen Bertha, and Augustine are all buried in the Abbey, which also houses the tombs of all the earliest archbishops of Canterbury, as well as the kings of Kent. There was growing rivalry between the abbey and the nearby cathedral, and after AD758 archbishops were buried in the latter.*

*By the Middle Ages, the abbey had grown into one of the greatest and richest monasteries in Europe, until it was largely destroyed in 1538 during the Dissolution of the Monasteries. The gilded shrine containing the remains of St Augustine was secretly removed, and for a time rested in St Mary's Church, Chilham (see walk 18).*

**Open all year, April to the end of September, 10am–6pm, October to March, 10am–4pm. There is an admission charge, but it is free to English Heritage members.**

- Continue along the road past the entrance to the Abbey. Turn right with the major road and then very shortly turn left down Church Street to St Pauls.
- At the end of Church Street cross the ring road at the pedestrian lights and pass through the city walls via Burgate.

*Burgate is the site of one of the eight gates that pierced the mediaeval city walls of Canterbury.*

- Pass the Cathedral Postern on your right and keep ahead up the cobbled street, passing the tower of St Mary Magdalene on your left.

*The tower of St Magdalenes' survived German bombing raids during World War Two and is now used to display some old memorial stones.*

- Ignore all turns to the left and follow the road to reach a square with a war memorial, in front of the Christ Church gate into the cathedral precinct.

*In AD602 an existing church, part of the palace of King Ethelbert, was given to Augustine as a place of worship. This was the start of the complex that was to become Canterbury Cathedral. The church was added to over the next two centuries, but was burnt to the ground when the Danes sacked Canterbury in 1011 and kidnapped Archbishop Alfege. Lanfranc, the first of the Norman archbishops, was consecrated in the ruins of the church in 1070 and immediately set about building a suitable cathedral, work continued by his successor Anselm.*

*The power and independence of the church brought it into increasing disagreement with the Crown. In an attempt to stop these disputes Henry II appointed his trusted friend and Chancellor Thomas Becket as Archbishop of Canterbury in 1162. Far from solving the problem, this appointment exacerbated it, for the previously worldly and loyal Becket now threw his considerable energies and intelligence into the cause of the church and rapidly came into conflict with the king. The archbishop was exiled in 1163, but allowed to return in 1170, only to be murdered in the cathedral by four of the king's barons. Henry's infamous remark 'What cowards have I about me, that no one will deliver me from this lowborn priest!', was taken as the order for the murder, although whether it was intended to be such is uncertain.*

*Becket was immediately regarded as a saint, not so much for what he was or had done but for the fact that he had been martyred for his faith. The cathedral became a place of pilgrimage almost at once. When a fire destroyed much of the building four years later, the work of reconstruction started yet again, but this time funded by money pouring in from pilgrims. The present cathedral, known technically as the Church of Christ Canterbury, dates largely from the period 1275–1400, although some remains of the earlier building can still be found, most notably the early Norman crypt. The crowning glory of the cathedral, the magnificent Bell Harry Tower, was not completed until 1496.*

*A complex of other buildings grew up within the cathedral grounds: infirmaries for sick travellers, hostels and lodgings of graded comfort for pilgrims, cloisters to accommodate increasing numbers of visitors and schools. One of the finest of these buildings, Meister Omers, is now used as a boarding dormitory for the King's School, which was founded by Henry VIII during the Reformation, to divert education from the hands of the Catholic church. The wealth and buildings of the cathedral were used to subsidise this project.*

*As well as the shrine to Thomas Becket (which was looted during the Reformation), the cathedral contains a number of tombs, the most notable of which is probably that of the Black Prince. Interestingly, although the major cathedral in England, only one English king, Henry IV, is buried here.*

**The cathedral complex and the cathedral itself contain architectural splendours far too numerous to list individually here. The complex can be visited, and the main entrance is via the Christ Church Gate. Currently the cathedral precinct charges an entrance fee to visitors.**

- Bear right past Christ Church Gate to reach a cross road, and turn right into Palace Street.
- Go down Palace Street, passing St Alfege's Church and Conquest House on the left.

The magnificent entrance to Canterbury Cathedral.

*St Alfege's is named after Canterbury's very own saint, Archbishop Alfege, who was carried off by the Danes in AD1012 for ransom and murdered by them at their camp in Greenwich after he refused to allow a ransom to be paid. It is Early English in style, and, although it is uncertain when it was actually built, it was described in 1166 as 'old'.*

- At a T-junction, turn right into The Borough and pass the entrance of King's School on your right.
- Where the ragstone wall of the school ends on your right, and opposite the Jolly Sailor Ale House, turn left down St Radigunds Street.

*This is the site of the north gate into Canterbury. You are following the course of the old city wall.*

- After 30 yards bear left past a sunken garden and follow the road across a junction and past The Dolphin on your right.
- Fifty yards after The Dolphin and just before a bridge turn half-left at the top of Mill Lane and go through a gate and over a footbridge across a weir.
- Follow the footpath over another footbridge crossing sluice gates and turn left to follow the path through a quiet garden along the side of the River Stour.

*The River Stour flows through the North Downs at Chilham (see walk 18) and has always been an important communications route leading into Canterbury. The old building on the river side in front of you is the remains of the Blackfriars, home to the Dominicans who came to Canterbury in 1237. Further up the river, not visible from here, is the Greyfriars, home to the Franciscans who had arrived 13 years before the Dominicans but did not have a permanent site for their friary until 1267. Both sets of friars were healing orders, who set up hospitals to tend the sick who were flocking into Canterbury in the hope of being cured at the shrine of St Thomas Becket.*

- Leave the garden by metal gates and turn left for five yards to reach a road.
- Turn right along the road for 100 yards to a T-junction, where you turn left.
- Follow the road as it curves left *(following the course of the old city wall again)* to reach Westgate.

*The Westgate is said to be the finest city gate in England. It was built in 1380 by Archbishop Simon, part of the massive city wall defences and the only one of the eight city gates to survive. For a time it served as a city gaol. The Westgate was the entrance into the city for all travellers from London. Pilgrims' coming to pay homage at the shrine of Thomas Becket would have entered Canterbury through this gate.*

- With your back to Westgate, go straight on down St Peter's Street.

*St Peter's Street was the main thoroughfare into the city, and in the Middle Ages it would have been lined with taverns, boarding houses for travellers and pilgrims, shops and stalls selling not only provisions but also religious relics and all the other paraphernalia of a mediaeval tourist town. If you look above the modern shop façades to the first-floor level you can still see that many of the buildings in this street are of great age, and it is not hard to imagine what it would have looked like 600 years ago.*

● Pass St Peter's Church on your left and, shortly after, the Weavers' House.

*St Peter's Church is an interesting little church. It is Norman with re-used red Roman bricks included in its construction. It is worthy of a brief visit.*

*The Weavers' House was built in 1561, although the mock half-timbering was added at a later stage. It was built as a refuge for Walloon and Huguenot weavers fleeing from the religious persecution that swept Flanders. Wool production and weaving was an important industry in Kent, and Canterbury was a major centre for the sale and despatch of woollen goods. The expertise that foreign refugees brought into the English woollen trade greatly enhanced Canterbury's position.*

● Pass Eastbridge Hospital on your right.

*Eastbridge Hospital was founded in 1190 as a hostel for poor pilgrims (the name 'hospital' has altered over the centuries and is today confusing as it is associated with the tending of the ill: 'hospice' would be a better translation of its meaning in the Middle Ages). It was built to accommodate pilgrims, many of them sick, who came to the shrine of St Thomas looking for a cure. They paid 4d (just over 1.5p) a night to stay there. It was also known as the Hospital of St Thomas the Martyr, and contains a Norman undercroft, some fine 12th and 13th-century frescoes and a chapel with a 13th-century roof. In the 16th century it became a charity school for poor boys, and later still it was turned into almshouses.*

● Fifty yards past Eastbridge Hospital, turn right down Stour Street.
● Follow Stour Street past modern buildings and past the Canterbury Heritage Centre on the right.

*The Heritage Centre is housed in the Poor Priests Hospital, built around 1200 by the Franciscan monks as a hospice for their members. It continued to be used until the reign of Elizabeth I, when it was given to the city for municipal use.*

● Continue straight on, ignoring side turns, down the quiet road.
● Pass a car park on your left and keep straight on up Church Lane to St Mildred's Church.

*St Mildred's was founded in the eighth century and is the oldest church within the city walls. The original church burnt down in 1246 and was replaced with the present building.*

● Pass left around St Mildred's. Exit via gates and turn left through metal posts and up a brick paved road to reach Canterbury Castle.

*All that remains of Canterbury Castle is the keep, the fifth largest in England. It was built partly of local flint, partly of recycled Roman bricks and stones, and faced in Kentish ragstone. It stands on a stepped plinth, 13 feet high and 6 feet wider than the keep itself and its high walls are reinforced with clasping buttresses. The keep was originally 80 feet high.*

*The first castle was a simple motte and bailey, a fort built upon an earthen mound and surrounded by a palisade. It was built by the Normans immediately after the Conquest in 1066 and was replaced in 1085 with a stone, three-storey castle. The castle had a permanent garrison of 15 knights and 40 foot sergeants, but with accommodation for many more in times of war.*

*Canterbury Castle never saw any fighting. It was captured without a struggle in 1216 by Louis, Dauphin of France, when he came to depose King John, but from then on was used as a prison. In 1277 Kentish Jews were held here before being deported. In 1380 the castle was attacked by Wat Tyler during the Peasants' Revolt against unfair royal taxation, when its inmates were released and the Sheriff forced to take the peasants' oath (see also walks 8 and 10). In 1539 the castle was involved in the religious disputes sweeping the country, when Archbishop Cranmer used the gaol to imprison two monks who objected to the dissolution of the monasteries. The castle ceased to be used in the 1590s, and by 1609 it was in ruins.*

● Follow the brick-paved road to reach a tarmacked road. Cross the road and walk up the footpath to right of car park. Pass the toilets and go up the ramp on to the city walls.

*Canterbury has been walled since Roman times. The present walls are mediaeval, totally encircled the city and were pierced by eight heavily fortified gates. In addition, there were 21 watch-towers at intervals. Todays walls have been restored and widened.*

● Walk along walls, passing Dane John Mound on your left.

*This mound was originally called the 'donjon' mound, the temporary site of a Norman keep-cum-prison tower (donjon being french for 'keep'). The name was anglicised to Dane John Mound, and it was surmounted by a monument in 1800 commemorating various civic reconstructions. The origin of the mound is far older, it being a burial mound used by the Romans but perhaps pre-dating even them.*

● Follow the wall, crossing Watling Street by a bridge and continuing along the restored and widened walls.

*The area of the city just to your left, that now contains the bus station, was devastated in June 1942 by German bombing raids, part of the so-called 'Baedeker' raids which specifically targeted sites of cultural or artistic interest, in retaliation for allied raids that had destroyed German historic cities. The cathedral itself, although a target, was missed.*

● Descend and cross St George Street.
● Follow the walls back to Burgate.
● Turn right through the gate and then turn left back to the car park.

## WALK 8
# Rochester: the Norman Conquest takes hold

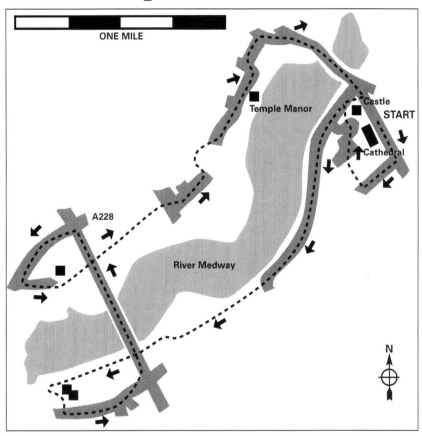

**Distance:** 7.5 miles

**Map:** OS sheet 178

**Start and Parking:** The walk starts from the War Memorial Garden in High Street, at the back of Rochester Cathedral (grid ref: 743685). The Northgate car park (pay and display) just off Corporation Street is the closest to the start, although there is plenty of other parking.

**Refreshments:** Public houses, shops, cafés and tearooms in Rochester. Public houses in Strood.

## Historical Background

For the new Norman monarchy, the overwhelming need in the first decades after the Conquest was to impress upon their Saxon subjects the superiority of Norman culture, and so nip any thoughts of revolt in the bud. Huge new castles and cathedrals were an obvious outward sign of this superiority, the one displaying a vigorous defence of the realm, the other an equally vigorous defence of the faith. Nowhere can this be better seen than in Rochester.

William the Conqueror arrived with an army of only 6,000, many of them mercenaries who had been dismissed by 1070. The Conquest was not followed by a mass influx of settlers into England and was essentially the exchange of one aristocracy for a indifferent one. William won a personal kingdom for himself and then held it by rewarding his followers with lands captured from the defeated Saxons. These Norman landowners now had a vested interest in defending their new estates.

The Norman's brought with them the art of castle building to England. William himself saw to it that a castle was built in every county town, and at points of strategic importance. His nobles were allowed a free hand to build private castles to defend their lands. In the years immediately following the Conquest a rash of castles sprang up over England.

The Norman's were also a genuinely devout people. The church followed the Norman army into England, and although churchmen were often powerful landowners in their own right, they also set about building churches, monasteries and huge cathedrals as an outward sign of their faith. This Norman ecclesiastical architecture was on a far grander scale than anything achieved by the Saxons.

Even today, when the city has many high modern buildings, the cathedral and especially the castle are prominent. In 1080, when Rochester was a cluster of one and two-storey buildings, most built of wood and wattle, the psychological effect of these two massive buildings upon the defeated Saxons must have been overwhelming.

## The Walk

**This walk goes around the old city of Rochester, where it passes several sites that are a reminder of Charles Dickens's association with the city as well as the cathedral and castle. It then goes down the banks of the River Medway, past the site of the most significant battle of Roman times in Kent, and returns via a fortified manor house established by the Knights Templar.**

● Standing in War Memorial Garden, with your back to the cathedral, turn right along the High Street.

*Rochester was a stronghold of the Belgae, a tribe settled in Britain with connections on both sides of the channel and Rome's traditional enemies. It commands an important strategic position at the Medway's lowest crossing point. After the defeat of the Belgae in AD43, the Romans built a huge fortified camp here, with walls enclosing 23 acres. Soon the city of Durobrivae grew up, astride Watling Street, the major Roman road in the province, which ran from Richborough and Dover to London. High Street is part of Watling Street.*

- In a few yards you will pass Watts Charity on your left.

*Watts Charity featured in Dickens's short story* The Seven Poor Travellers. *It is an Elizabethan boarding house, set up in 1579 by Richard Watt, MP for Rochester, to provide free board and lodging for six poor travellers. It continued to do so until 1939.*

- Pass Eagle Close on your right, with the old city wall visible on your right. (It is worth detouring down Eagle Court to have a closer view of the wall.)

*The mediaeval town walls followed the course of earlier Roman ones. This part has survived to its full height, complete with battlements.*

- Opposite the Dickens centre, turn right up Crow Lane.

*Charles Dickens came to Rochester in 1817, at the age of five, when his father moved from Portsmouth to work in Chatham Dockyard, and he lived here much of his life. In 1856 Dickens bought Gads Hill Place, in nearby Higham, which became his home for most of his latter years and is where he died in 1870. Dickens loved Rochester and nearby Chatham, and the Medway towns feature in many of his novels, in particular* Great Expectations *and* The Pickwick Papers. *It was Dickens's wish to be buried in Rochester Cathedral, but Queen Victoria decreed he should instead be buried in Westminster Cathedral.*

*The Charles Dickens centre contains a wealth of memorabilia, including his 'Swiss Chalet', a garden house from Gads Hill where he did much of his later work.*

**Open daily 10am–6pm. Admission fee.**

- Fifty yards past the entrance to King's School on the right, turn right into a park.

*On the opposite side of the road is Restoration House, where Charles II stayed in 1661 on his return to England, en route for London and his Coronation. It features in Dickens's* Great Expectations *as the home of Miss Havisham.*

- Bear right with the path and exit into a road. Turn right down the road, passing Oriel House on the right.

*Look for the two firemarks on Oriel House: these were 18th-century metal plates that identified the companies who had insured the house against fire. Insurance companies provided their own fire service and would only fight the blaze in properties that could be identified as being insured with them!*

- At the bottom of the road turn left, walking down Minor Canon Row.

The Norman cathedral at Rochester was started in 1077.

*Minor Canon Row was built in 1723 as homes for minor clergy. It features in Dickens's* The Mystery of Edwin Drood.

- In 50 yards turn right at a T-junction and follow the road to the entrance of the cathedral.

*The original cathedral in Rochester was founded in 604 by Ethelbert, King of Kent, for Justus, the first Bishop of Rochester, after the diocese had been founded by St Augustine. It was finally laid to waste by the Vikings. The foundations of the Saxon cathedral are visible outside the north door of the present cathedral.*

*In 1077 Gundulph, a monk from Bec in Normandy, was made Bishop of Rochester. This appointment was as much political as religious and Gundulph was a major landowner, with many holdings in Kent, including Rochester, Canterbury and Malling (see walk 9). In 1082 Gundulph, at the order of his patron Lanfranc Archbishop of Canterbury, set about building a new cathedral that would be a visible symbol of Norman wealth, piety and power. Gundulph was associated with a number of major building works in the first years after the Conquest: as well as Rochester Cathedral he supervised the building of Rochester Castle and the hub of the Tower of London, the White Tower. Gundulph was not an architect, but appears to have been a knowledgeable administrator who knew how to get good work done. Rochester Cathedral is England's second oldest cathedral, after Canterbury, and part of the crypt, the nave and the magnificent West Portal are original Norman.*

- Facing the castle with your back to the cathedral entrance, turn left and walk around the castle, keeping the curtain wall on your right.
- Enter the castle via a gate in the curtain wall and walk forward to the wooden steps giving access to the keep.

*Such was the strategic importance of Rochester that the Normans erected their first castle in the year following the Conquest. It was built by Odo, Bishop of Bayeaux, William's troublesome half-brother. In 1082 Odo rebelled against William and was briefly imprisoned. He recovered from this disgrace but in 1087, on William's death, supported William's son Robert against King William Rufus, the Conqueror's younger son and designated successor to the English throne. Rochester became a headquarters for the unsuccessful rebellion and was besieged and rapidly captured by the king. Odo was exiled, later to die on the first crusade.*

*After the siege, the king demanded that Bishop Gundulph supervise and pay for a much stronger castle at Rochester, in return for being confirmed as owner of the manor of Haddenham in Buckinghamshire. Gundulph duly greatly strengthened the curtain walls, towers and gatehouse.*

*Rochester was a royal, not a private, castle, but Henry I, William Rufus's successor, granted custody of Rochester Castle to the Archbishopric of Canterbury. It was during this period, in 1126, that the keep was constructed. It is the tallest Norman keep in England, standing over 100 feet high, with walls 12 feet thick and measuring 160 yards by 130 yards. However, a royal castle under the custody of some other lord is a potentially dangerous state of affairs, for*

**Rochester Castle, built by the Normans to impose their rule in England.**

*in 1215 Archbishop Langton, ever an enemy to King John, allowed the castle to be held against the king during the barons' rebellion. John recaptured the castle after a three-month siege. John's successor, Henry III, rebuilt and further strengthened the castle and took it back into royal hands, and it was thereafter controlled by a constable responsible solely to the king.*

*In 1264 Rochester Castle was besieged for a third time, by Simon de Montfort, during the Barons' rebellion against King Henry III. Although the attackers broke through the curtain wall into the bailey, the defenders successfully held the keep against all attack.*

*The defences of the castle and the town were further strengthened during the 14th century, for Rochester defended both the Medway and the land approaches to London against French raids during the Hundred Years War. In 1381 the castle was attacked for a fourth time, this time by Wat Tyler's forces during the Peasants' Revolt, when the townspeople of Rochester aided the rebels in the capture of the castle (for the Peasants' Revolt, see also walks 7 and 10).*

*By the end of the 14th century Rochester's fortifications were at their strongest, but the strategic importance of the castle was passing and Rochester Castle did not see action again.*

**Rochester Castle is open April to September, 10am–6pm, October to March, 10am–4pm. There is an admission charge, but it is free to members of English Heritage.**

● Leave the keep and walk half-right down a broad gravel path to a bastion with a cannon, overlooking the road bridge.

● Leave the castle by descending a broad flight of steps onto the junction of Esplanade and Castle Hill.

● Cross the road to the river front and turn left. After 80 yards turn right into some riverside gardens. Turn left and walk alongside the Medway, passing the marina.

- Continue ahead through an open area to reach a road, keeping roughly parallel with the river front.
- On reaching the road turn right. Follow the road until it reaches the river again and continue ahead along the riverside walk.
- Follow the road for half a mile. Where the road turns left, just after passing warehouses on the left, keep straight on to a footpath into Batys Marsh Nature Reserve.
- Follow the path, with fences on the left and the river off to the right. Ignore a left turn at a barrier but keep straight ahead down a clear path.
- Follow the footpath out to a road. Keep ahead, descending with the road and passing the gates to Beacon Boat Yard.
- At the entrance to the Medway Bridge Marina, go ahead up the footpath to the left of the gates.
- Keep ahead along an enclosed footpath for 200 yards, keeping the fence to the marina on your right and ignoring a waymarked path off to the left.
- Where the marina fence turns right, cross a stile and turn right down to the river bank. Turn left along the foreshore.
- Pass a jetty on the right and keep straight on to cross a stile and enter an enclosed footpath.
- Follow the footpath under the Medway Bridge and keep straight on along the riverbank.
- Follow the path out to a track. Keep ahead and pass through a metal kissing gate beside a field gate. Keep ahead along the track.
- Where the track ends keep ahead along a narrow footpath for 30 yards and climb onto the embankment.
- Do not follow the clear path along the top of the embankment, but descend and bear left on a grassy path through shrubland.
- Follow the path as it swings left towards a row of houses.
- Go through a gate to the houses. At a fork in 10 yards, go left to pass along the front of the houses.
- Opposite the last house, go through a gap in the wall on the right and down some steps to enter a field.
- Go half-right across the field to reach a drive.
- Turn left up the drive for five yards to a road, and then turn left along the road for a third of a mile.
- Just after passing Nashenden Farm Lane on the right, and 30 yards before the bridge, turn left up a track to reach the walkway alongside the road over the bridge.
- Cross the Medway bridge but pause halfway across and look down at the river.

*This is the site of the only major battle fought in Kent against the Romans when they invaded Britain in AD43. The Medway has not altered a great deal since that battle and it is possible to look out and down and picture the scene.*

*Following Caesar's two expeditions a century before, the Emperor Claudius launched a full-blown invasion of Britain. Four full legions and auxiliaries, nearly 50,000 men in total, landed at Richborough (see walk 4). Although the Britons had intelligence of their arrival, the Romans landed later in the campaigning season than expected and the British army, mainly tribal irregulars, had dispersed to bring in the harvest. In consequence the Roman landing was unopposed and the legions thrust northwards through Kent, while the Britons hastily re-assembled their army.*

*A British army of 60–80,000 men drew up on the western bank of the Medway (to your right as you look down), just downstream of where you are standing, confident that the river would provide a defensive barrier to the Roman legions drawn up on the east (left) bank. However, the Roman army included auxiliary troops from the Batavi tribe in Holland, experienced at swimming fully armed. These swam the river just in front of you and attacked the Britons on their flank. While the Britons turned to face this attack, a Roman legion was able to flounder its way across the shingle banks and mudflats further downstream and establish a bridgehead. Although strongly counter-attacked, the Romans poured their remaining legions across the river to reinforce their comrades, and after two days of fighting routed the British forces.*

*This battle was the most decisive action in the whole Roman invasion. Never again would the Romans be opposed in Kent, which soon settled down to become the most affluent and Romanised part of the new province of Britannia.*

- At the far end of the bridge follow the footpath up to the A228.
- Turn left and walk down the left-hand side of the A228 for half a mile, crossing a railway bridge and passing the entrance to a recycling centre.
- One hundred yards past the recycling centre, turn left down a tarmacked lane.
- Descend the lane and pass between houses. Where the tarmacked lane ends, turn right down a drive and just before the railway, turn left to pass to the right of a house.
- Follow an enclosed footpath for 15 yards, and then keep straight on along the bottom edge of the field, with the railway on your immediate right.
- Cross the stile at the field end and keep straight on along the next field, passing under the Medway bridge to a stile. Pass through a narrow band of trees and bear half-right up to the field.
- Maintain the same line direction along the next field, now with the field boundary on the right, and follow out onto a road.
- Cross the road and keep ahead down Norman Close.
- At the end of Norman Close keep ahead up a footpath to the left of metal factory gates. Follow the footpath around to the left, keeping iron railings on your right, as it passes between industrial units.
- At the end of the units climb and turn right, now with a railway on your left.
- Do not cross the railway bridge but keep straight on down an enclosed footpath, with the railway on your left.
- Turn right and follow the path, now concrete and gently stepped, down between fences and out to a road.
- Turn left along the road, ignoring side turnings. In 350 yards, pass a pillar box on the left at a road junction. Thirty yards later, pass Temple Manor on the right.

*Temple Manor is a 13th-century hall built to provide lodgings for the Knights Templar as they journeyed to or from the Holy Land. The Templars were a military religious order founded around AD1118, when Hughes de Payen and eight other knights banded together to protect pilgrims en route to Jerusalem. Their original headquarters were on top of the Temple mound in Jerusalem, hence 'Templars'.*

*The order soon gained papal approval and rapidly grew in numbers and wealth. The loss of the Latin Kingdoms, modern-day Palestine, forced the order to relocate to the West, where they established themselves as bankers to the various monarchs. Their independence and wealth made them arrogant and they eventually became hated by both clergy and secular authorities. In 1307 the order was attacked by Philip IV of France, who seized Templar land and property and accused the order of heresy. Pope Clement V was bullied into issuing a papal edict dissolving the order. Although the Templars continued to exist in England, Germany and Spain for some years after their expulsion from France, they never regained their former influence and power, and, as the Holy Land ceased to be a major issue in European politics, the order gradually withered away. (Another Templar property can be seen at West Peckham, walk 17.)*

- Continue along the road for another 350 yards, ignoring side turnings. The road, called Knights Road in memory of the Templars, turns sharp left and 30 yards later reaches a more major road at a give way sign.
- Turn right down the major road. At a T-junction, turn right down Commercial Road and follow the road under a railway bridge.
- Keep ahead along the right-hand pavement. Pass a subway entrance and keep ahead. Do not go onto the bridge but keep forward to the riverfront for a fine view of the castle and part of the town wall across the river.
- Climb steps onto the bridge and cross the river.

*This bridge was built in 1857, but the Medway has been bridged at this point since Roman times. The present bridge replaced a mediaeval one, built between 1383 and 1393. It had crenellated towers at each end as part of the defences of Rochester, and a drawbridge between its piers to allow tall ships access to the sheltered and protected Medway. This mediaeval bridge was so well built that 400 years later gunpowder was needed to demolish it.*

- At the end of the bridge cross The Esplanade and keep ahead. Cross Gundolph Street on the right.

*The corner of Gundolph Street marks the position of Rochester's old North Gate and is the site of the Crown Inn, the first and one of the most affluent inns travellers would encounter on entering the city. Anne of Cleves stayed there en route for her Coronation.*

- Keep ahead up High Street to return to War Memorial Gardens on your right.

*Look out for the Guildhall on your left as you enter High Street, built in 1687 and one of the finest 17th-century civic buildings in Kent.*

WALK 9

# West Malling: Norman feudalism in action

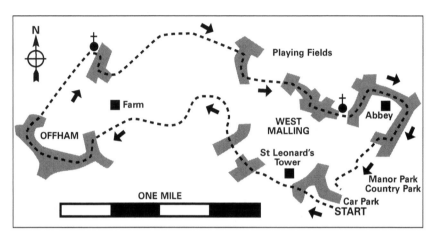

**Distance:** 5 miles

**Map:** OS sheet 178 or 188

**Start and Parking:** The walk starts from Manor Park Country Park (grid ref: 679571) at the southern end of West Malling, which is itself just south of the junction of the A20 and the A228, 10 miles east of Sevenoaks and six miles west of Maidstone. The country park is signposted from both A roads.

**Refreshments:** Public houses, tearooms and shops in West Malling, public house in Offham.

### Historical Background

The area of West Malling and Offham were once largely part of the estates of Gundulph, Bishop of Rochester. They were given to Gundulph shortly after the Norman Conquest by King William, an extensive area of rich agricultural land which was soon to be organised in accordance with Norman feudalism.

When William the Conqueror seized the English Crown he brought with him a concept new to English thought, the theory that all land was the king's by right, and that land was held by others only by the king's gift, and in return for specified services. This service was initially military, since the king needed to ensure that his new subjects were properly subdued and that his new realm could be protected without the Crown bearing the cost of a standing army. The king held all the privileges of monarchy in return for swearing to defend his subjects against attack

74

and granted land to his barons and to the clergy, who in turn were expected to provide arms and men to fight when required. These great landowners granted land to their knights in return for military service when required, and so on down through all strata of society.

Gundulph organised his estates along these lines, with holdings of land being granted to lesser landlords in return for military service. He also set about developing his holdings, in a display of Norman power and wealth designed to overawe his Saxon vassals. An abbey was established at East Malling, the Saxon church was redeveloped and extended, and a fortified keep built to protect and impress the manor.

**The Walk**
**This walk passes the ruins of Gundulph's keep and the abbey he established, and goes through woods and farmland to visit Offham, whose village green and quintain give a strong reminder of its feudal past.**

- Standing facing the access road to the car park, take the waymarked footpath to the left of the road. Follow the path alongside the road.
- Descend to the access road and go forward for a few yards. Just before the bridge turn left down a waymarked path to reach a lane.
- Follow the lane past cottages to the main road. Cross the road to the track opposite, and go up past the tower.

*St Leonard's Tower was built around 1100 as a fortified keep by Gundulph, Bishop of Rochester from 1077–1108, who was also responsible for the building of Rochester Cathedral and Castle (see walk 8). Gundulph had extensive holdings of land across Kent (see also walk 1) and the area around West Malling was especially important to him. This tower is the keep of a small fortified manor house, built by the Archbishop partly as an occasional residence but also as a base from which to protect his lands. It would normally have been manned by a very small garrison, but provided the facilities to act as a base for a much larger force in times of troubles. The base of the tower is made from tufa, a volcanic stone favoured by the Normans in their fortifications, and the outline of the walls of a small chapel can still just be distinguished adjoining the tower.*

- Continue along a fenced track. Pass through a gate and continue along the track to join a tarmacked farm drive. Follow the drive to a road.
- Turn half-left across the road and go down a track between buildings. The track soon becomes a footpath. Follow this out to a lane.
- Cross the lane and cross a stile opposite, then 'turn right and walk down the field edge, alongside the lane. Cross a drive and keep ahead along the side of the field, still with a hedge and field on the right.
- Swing left with the path. At a junction of tracks keep ahead. Do not enter the wood along a waymarked path but instead take the path to the left, passing the wood on your right.

- Keep ahead along the edge of the field, with trees on your right. Where the trees swing away to the right, keep straight on, keeping the field on your left.
- At the field end, turn left and follow the field boundary, still with the field on your left and now with a hedge on your right.
- At a farm track, turn right through a gap and then immediately turn left. Go ahead down the next field, maintaining the same direction but now with the hedge on your left.
- Follow the hedge right and then left. Where the hedge ends, turn right at a waymarked post and follow the path across the middle of a field, aiming at a red roof seen ahead.
- At a T-junction with a track, in the middle of the field and 100 yards short of the red roof, turn left.
- In another 100 yards, at another T-junction of tracks, keep straight on along a footpath across the field, aiming for trees seen ahead.
- At the field edge cross a stile and keep straight on down an enclosed footpath to reach a road by an ex-public house.
- Keep ahead down the road (Church Road) for a few yards, to a T-junction with Teston Road. Turn right up Teston Road, soon to reach the village green of Offham with its quintain.

*'Tilting' was a popular sport from Roman times, and came to prominence in England with the arrival of the Normans. The quintain is a two-armed post which pivots around a central pole. It would have a target fixed on one arm and a heavy sandbag on the other. A horseman would ride at the quintain, aiming to strike the target, thus causing the quintain to spin, and then avoid being struck by the sandbag.*

Quintains were used in the Middle Ages for 'tilting'. This one, on the village green at Offham, is the only one left in England.

*Although a sport enjoyed at festive times, the origin of the quintain has a serious military purpose, being to teach the art of fighting on horseback. Knights were the most wealthy and powerful men in a manor, and were required to provide their lord with military service for a specified number of days each year, 40 days a year in times of peace and 60 days in times of war. They were also required to undergo a number of days training per year. The quintain was a popular training tool, although they would have been located in the castles where the knights lived and worked, not on village greens.*

*The quintain at Offham is the only one in England. It is not original, but is periodically replaced.*

*As an aside, the less affluent populace were required to do their military service as foot soldiers, armed with a pike and, by the 14th century, the deadly English longbow. These people too were required to train, in their case with the bow for an hour every Sunday after the church service had finished. Their training ground was the archery butts, and many older English towns and villages still have a street named 'The Butts' in consequence.*

- Continue to follow the road, passing the Kings Head public house. Fifty yards past the pub turn right down Pepingstraw Close.
- Where the road bends right, keep straight on up a footpath, at a concrete footpath sign and passing a horse barrier.
- Follow the footpath into woods. At a fork, keep right on the path following the edge of woods.
- When the path reaches a field keep straight on down a tree-lined path, with a field on your right.
- Emerge from the trees and keep ahead to farm buildings.
- Pass a barn on your right. At a T-junction turn right and follow the drive out to the road beside Offham Church.
- Turn right down the road, 50 yards past the church, opposite Church Farm, turn left up a drive.
- Where the hedge on the left ends and the drive emerges into an open field, turn half-left and follow the footpath across the field, aiming for woods seen ahead.
- At trees (an outlier of the wood) and a marker post, cross farm tracks and continue along the same line into the woods ahead.
- Enter the woods and follow a broad footpath through trees.
- At the end of the woods emerge into field at a junction of tracks. Do not cross a stile but keep ahead down the field, with a fence on the left and West Malling seen ahead.
- Follow the path to a stile at a junction of roads. Do not go down Norman Road, but turn sharp right up the lane.
- Follow the lane for 250 yards and around a left bend. Pass steps descending the bank on the right and immediately turn left onto a footpath along the side of a field.
- Go along the right-hand side of the field and keep ahead down an enclosed footpath, now with a recreation field on the left.
- At the end of the recreation field, follow a tarmacked path between garden fences and out to a road.

- Cross the road and continue down the path between garden fences to reach another road
- Keep ahead along this road (Epsom Close), ignoring a footpath on the left in a few yards, and crossing Sandown Road in 60 yards.
- At a T-junction turn right, passing between garages, and 50 yards later turn left along the road.
- At a crossroads in 50 yards time, keep ahead down Churchfields.
- Where the road bends, keep straight on up a footpath, with the road behind the hedge on the left, aiming for the church spire seen ahead.
- At the end of the footpath keep ahead and follow an alley into the churchyard.
- Follow the path past the church and out to the road.

*The church of St Mary the Virgin is Norman in origin, with a 19th-century spire, and an Early English chancel with fine Jacobean alabaster tombs. It has a James II coat of arms, possibly carved by Grinling Gibbons, a famous carver of wood and stone who collaborated with Sir Christopher Wren. Some of Gibbons's work can be seen in Hampton Court.*

- Turn left up the main road and pass through the Market Square.

*West Malling has been an affluent market town for many centuries, and its wide market square is flanked by houses from Elizabethan, Jacobean and Georgian times.*

- At a white-painted outfitters shop, turn right down Swan Street. In 200 yards pass St Mary's Abbey on your right.

*The original Abbey of East Malling was part of the holdings of Gundulph, Bishop of Rochester, and protected by his nearby keep, St Leonard's Tower. This abbey was destroyed in 1190, along with most of the old village, and rebuilt as a nunnery. Part of the original Norman building still remains, now incorporated into the later building. It is still used as such today, being shared between the Benedictine nuns and the Cistercian order.*

- Proceed for a further 200 yards past the Abbey gate, looking our for Sluice exit in the wall on the right. Turn right down Lavenders Road, following the wall of the Abbey.
- In 300 yards turn right into Water Lane, and 50 yards later turn left through a kissing gate into Manor Park Country Park.
- Keep straight on along a broad grassy track. At a fork in 60 yards, drop down right to the lakeside.
- Turn left and walk with the lake on your right.

*The Manor House seen across the lake is Douce House, once home of Thomas Douce, whose 18th-century estate included all the land that is now Manor Park. The house is now owned by Commercial Union as a training centre.*

- At the end of the lake, turn left up the access drive back to the car park.

# WALK 10
# Appledore: raiders and traders in the Middle Ages

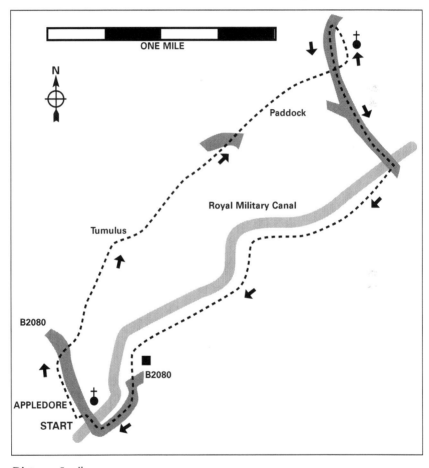

**Distance:** 5 miles

**Map:** OS sheet 189

**Start and Parking:** The walk commences from Appledore Church (grid ref: 958292). Appledore is on the B2080, six miles south-east of Tenterden. There is road-side parking in the middle of Appledore village.

**Refreshments:** Public houses, tearoom and shop in Appledore.

**Historical Background**

Today Appledore is nine miles from the sea, but until the end of the 14th century it was a busy port. The area that is now Romney Marsh was then all sea, and the low coastline behind it a maze of creeks and estuaries winding through sandbanks and reedbeds. These estuaries provided sheltered anchorages facing the channel and the lucrative continental trade. Appledore was at the head of a tidal creek formed by the River Rother winding its way to the sea at Romney.

The period of Appledore's affluence was from about AD1100 to about AD1400. It was the home port for a flotilla of vessels that carried English wool and linen to France and returned with wines, silk, lace and all manner of other luxury goods. It also had a busy ship-building industry. The town flourished for 300 years, before the silting up of the Rother estuary cut the port off from the sea and Appledore gradually faded into obscurity.

Proximity to the channel and to Europe was a source of danger as well as prosperity. The remote coastline with its many secluded inlets and poor land communications was vulnerable to attack by England's enemies, and the wealth of the town brought it problems during the periods of social unrest in the Middle Ages. Even before there was a town at Appledore the Vikings had realised the strategic importance of the location and used it as a base for a year-long raid, in AD893–94. In 1380, during the Hundred Years War, the French raided this coast, sacking Appledore and burning the town. The following year, the ordinary people of Appledore were swept along in the Peasants' Revolt against the inequalities of society and attacked their wealthy neighbours before marching on London. The following century, governmental corruption was blamed for the decline in fortunes in the area, and the people of Appledore joined the campaign for better government led by Jack Cade (see walk 14).

In the 19th century the threat posed by Napoleon Bonaparte brought Romney Marsh and Appledore back into the front line, and the Royal Military Canal was built to provide a defence against invasion.

**The Walk**

**This walk follows the line of the coast during Appledore's mediaeval heyday. It passes various sites that reflect the town's history as a port and the raids made upon it over the centuries. It returns along the Royal Military Canal.**

- Walk up the main street of Appledore away from the canal and in the direction of Tenterden, passing the Swan Hotel on your right.

*Appledore has many fine old buildings, some dating back to the 14th century, homes of local merchants and ship-owners. The splendour of these houses speaks of the affluence of this tiny town in the past.*

- Eventually you will reach some playing fields on your right, opposite the entrance to Magpie Farm.

- Enter the playing fields beside the toilet block at a footpath sign.
- Cross the sports field diagonally, aiming for a gate in the top left-hand corner.
- Go through the gate and turn left along the field edge, with houses and a field beyond.
- In 200 yards, turn half-right across the field, aiming for a prominent oak tree in the far right corner.
- In the corner, cross a stile and footbridge. Go half-left across the next field, aiming for a stile ahead.
- Cross the stile and continue half-left across the next field, continuing the same line of advance and aiming at a tumulus seen on the skyline ahead.

*The tumulus is a round barrow dating from the Bronze Age, and was used to bury the cremated ashes of one man or at most one family, presumably a person or persons of importance. The barrow is a small round stone chamber, buried beneath a mound of earth. At the time it was constructed, all the flat lands to your right would have been beneath the sea, the gentle slopes ahead and to the left would have probably been densely wooded, with an area of marshy reeds and sandbanks up which you are walking. The tumulus would have stood, lonely and prominent, on this desolate shoreline.*

- Cross the top of the tumulus.

*Ahead and to the left are the chimneys of Hornes Place. The original house was destroyed during the Peasants' Revolt. In 1381 the government of King Richard II, desperate for revenue, levied the third poll tax in four years. This one was quite the harshest, and well beyond the means of most peasants to pay. Tax collectors were assaulted, attempts to enforce the law provoked resistance, and the countryside of Kent and Essex erupted into mutiny. In Kent this Peasants' Revolt was led by Wat Tyler, whose force marched through the county, ever increasing in numbers as it swept towards London. The peasants of Appledore rose up, attacked the local squire, William Horne, and burnt his home, Hornes Place, to the ground, before joining the revolt (see also walks 7 and 8 for the Peasants' Revolt in Kent).*

*As a footnote, the rebels reached the capital where they were joined by the London mob. King Richard in person met with the leaders and made them promises in return for their laying down their arms. These promises were rapidly broken, the leaders executed, and throughout the county, Appledore included, there was massive and savage retribution upon all those involved in the revolt.*

- Continuing the same line of advance, descend to a stile ahead on the field edge. Do not cross the stile but turn half-right to go down the field, with a line of trees on your left.
- At the end of the line of trees, continue half-left across the next large field. As you cross the summit of the field a gate will come into sight in line ahead of you.
- Go through this gate, at a waymark, and continue the same line of advance across the next field, aiming between two trees standing like goalposts on the far side.
- Cross a plank footbridge between these two trees and continue the same line of advance across a third field, to reach a stile beside a footpath sign, leading onto a road.

- Cross the road and enter the field opposite, beside a concrete footpath sign. Go half-right across this field, keeping well to the left of a clump of trees seen standing in the field ahead, and aiming just to the right of a telegraph pole. Soon a stile comes into sight in the trees ahead.
- Cross the stile and descend some steps to a second stile. Ignore a cross track, go over a second stile and climb the bank to a third stile, leading into a small paddock.
- Keep ahead along the right-hand edge of the paddock to cross a stile into a large field.
- Effectively you want to go more or less straight across this field. Initially, keep straight on along the edge of the field, keeping the field boundary to your right. Where the hedge ends, go quarter-right to the corner of the hedge seen ahead. Follow this hedge on your right hand for 250 yards. Where the hedge goes sharp right at a waymarker, aim half-left to a stile seen opposite.
- Cross the stile and turn left for 10 yards to cross a stile on the right.
- Go ahead, following the left-hand edge of the field around corners to reach a church.

*In the ninth century this spot was a headland overlooking a creek, a main channel of the River Rother. The Vikings sailed across the North Sea and up the English Channel from Denmark, up the creek from Romney to this easily-defended headland. Here they built a fortified encampment in AD893 from which to raid the surrounding countryside. The Vikings were persuaded to leave by King Alfred, rather than face a pitched battle, but not before they had spent a year on this coast, raiding with a fleet of 250 longships.*

*A church was built upon this spot to commemorate Alfred's victory, enlarged in 1170 when the tower was built. In 1380 the French raided this coastline during the Hundred Years War and burnt the church at the same time as sacking Appledore. The church was rebuilt, but the tower was struck by lightning in 1559, and the subsequent fire burnt the rest of the church again. The building was rebuilt but is now only used on occasions.*

- Follow the left-hand edge of the churchyard to cross a drive at a parking area to a stile ahead.
- Cross the stile and keep straight on across the field to a second stile.
- Cross this stile and the corner of a field to another stile 10 yards ahead. Cross this stile and descend some steps to a lane.
- Turn left up the lane.

*If you look to your left you will see the rocky outcrop which formed the promontory upon which the church was built.*

- After half a mile, turn left at a T-junction.
- Go down the lane for a quarter of a mile to cross the Royal Military Canal via a road bridge. Immediately on the other side of the bridge turn right into a parking area.
- Go through the parking area to a stile leading onto the canal bank. Keep along the bank, with the canal on your right, for nearly two miles.

In 1803 this coastline was again threatened by the French; however, not a mere raid this time but a full invasion by the armies of Napoleon. The first line of defence was to be a line of forts, called Martello Towers (see walk 22), along the coast itself. Inland of this was to be a canal, running for 23 miles along the inland edge of Romney Marsh, to provide a fall-back line of defence. The ability to combine infantry, cavalry and artillery into one devastating combined attack was what had given the French mastery on battlefields across Europe. The canal was built to disrupt this ability, by forcing any advance to be made piecemeal. Artillery and cavalry would be unable to cross, and infantry would be unlikely to get across without swimming, which would render their muskets useless.

As you will clearly see as you walk along, the canal was built in a series of zigzags, and every quarter of a mile, on each corner and at intervals between, a gun emplacement was built. These would provide interlocking fields of fire which would devastate any enemy trying to cross. In addition, a service road was built along the far side, which would enable troops to be moved quickly to any spot where the enemy did manage to cross.

As a further defence, sluice gates were built at intervals into the canal, to allow the low-lying Romney Marsh on your left to be flooded if necessary, thereby further disrupting an enemy invader. Some of these can still be spotted as you walk along, since many were refurbished in 1940, to be used to counter any German invasion.

The canal was finished in 1809, but by that time the threat of invasion had receded and it was never used.

● Eventually pass a pumping station on your left and follow the concrete track out to a road.
● Turn right along the road for a quarter of a mile to reach Appledore Bridge. Turn right across the bridge.

The Royal Military Canal, built as a defence against Napoleonic invasion.

*To the left across the bridge you will see a pillbox, dating from World War Two. In 1940–41 there was the threat of invasion by Nazi Germany, when again this region of Kent was seen as a likely landing spot. The 19th-century gun emplacements were replaced by the 20th-century equivalent.*

● Continue up main street back to your car, passing the church on your right.

*The original church in Appledore was Saxon, enlarged by the Normans. In 1380 the French raided up Rother Creek and devastated the land around. Appledore was sacked and burnt, and the church was destroyed. It was rebuilt after the raid, with a view to also providing a secure refuge in case of further attacks. The walls were built to almost fortress proportions, the tower enlarged, and the nave and north aisle built as a single unit, thereby providing a large open space for people seeking sanctuary. (Other examples of this style of fortress church can be seen in Sandwich: see walk 4.) The grandeur of the church, disproportionate to the size of Appledore today, speaks of the towns former wealth. In front of the church was the wide marketplace, in use until the last century.*

WALK 11

# Old Soar: mediaeval manors and Civil War churches

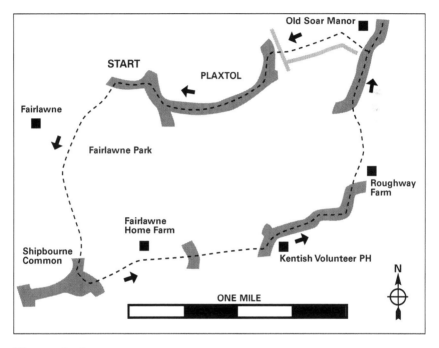

**Distance:** 5 miles

**Map:** OS sheet 188

**Start and parking:** The walk commences from the church at Plaxtol (grid ref: 602537). Plaxtol is on a minor road, one mile to the east of the A227 Tonbridge to Ightham road, five miles north of Tonbridge. There is on-street parking in Plaxtol, down side roads leading off the main street.

**Refreshments:** Shops and public houses in Plaxtol. Public house at Shipbourne. Public house at Dunks Green.

### Historical Background

In the Middle Ages the majority of Kent, Surrey and Sussex was covered by the huge Wealdan forest, a vast expanse of woodland with only scattered communities living in its clearings and with few roads winding through the dark trees. A livelihood was scratched out based on agriculture. Fields were cleared for growing wheat and grazing cattle and the all-prevailing forest offered timber, firewood, charcoal and summer acorns for pigs, the main livestock. Living in the forest was a hazardous business. The forest provided a refuge for outlaws and bandits as well as a hunting ground for common thieves, who preyed upon the small isolated communities as well as the few travellers along the often empty roads.

Law enforcement was often a local matter, with the lord of the manor responsible for adjudicating the less serious disputes among the local peasants and the Manor House often serving as a manorial court house. The lord also had to look to his own resources to defend himself, his family and his property against outlaws and robbers who roamed the forest, looking for easy pickings.

Old Soar Manor House was built in 1290 as a defensive home for the local lord of the manor and is one of the best examples of a mediaeval fortified manor house in England.

## The Walk

**The walk starts in Plaxtol and passes one of the very few churches to be built in England during the Commonwealth, as well as the home of a leading parliamentarian of that period. It then passes through orchards to visit Old Soar Manor House.**

● With the war memorial at your back and the church on your right, walk up Plaxtol Lane, passing a row of weatherboarded cottages on your right.

*Plaxtol church is very unusual in that it was built in 1649, during the Commonwealth. The king had been executed, Parliament ruled England, and Puritanism in its many forms set the style for religious observance. As a consequence of the puritan beliefs, Plaxtol church is not dedicated to any saint. In the south transept there is a Cromwellian carved screen, portraying the Crossing of the Red Sea, with both Israelites and Egyptians in 17th-century costume. The churchyard contains gravestones of a style unique to the Kent–Sussex border, with head-shaped humps carved with skulls. The church has a magnificent hammerbeam roof.*

● Continue along the road, now with the wall of Fairlawne Estate on your left. After 250 yards turn left across a stile into the estate.
● NB. There is no visible path across the estate grounds. However, there is a public right of way which is easy to keep to if the instructions are followed.
● With your back to the stile go straight across the park for 100 yards, aiming for a marker post in front of some ornate gates.

*These gates, seemingly standing in the middle open parkland, are the back entrance to Fairlawne Manor. A drive leads from the park to the house and provided access to it for riding. The gateway is magnificent, and offers an imposing façade to the house when seen from across the park.*

● From the marker post, head half-right around the gateway and then aim for a clump of four mature trees standing 50 yards ahead.

- From these trees, another marker post can now be seen down the slope, 200 yards away along your same line of advance. Pass to the left of a clump of six mature trees, to the right of an enclosure of new trees, to reach the marker post.
- From this post, keep straight on to a stile 75 yards ahead.
- Cross the stile and continue on the same line to a third marker post, seen ahead.

*Looking back and right you get your best view of Fairlawne. The Manor was built mainly in the 17th century, with later additions, and was the home of the Vane family. Sir Henry Vane, one-time governor of Massachusetts, was a close friend of Oliver Cromwell and a prominent parliamentarian during the years leading up to the Civil War. During the Commonwealth he was a radical reformer and became an outspoken critic of Cromwell, whom he viewed as having betrayed the revolution. With the Restoration of the monarchy, Sir Henry was tried for treason and was executed on Tower Hill, London, in June 1662. His headless corpse is buried in Plaxtol church, and his ghost is claimed to walk the grounds in the company of his wife, on the anniversary of his death!*

- At the third marker post, head half-left from your previous line of advance. Soon a fourth marker post becomes visible ahead, leading you down to a gate in the park corner, heading into trees.
- Pass through this gate and descend to a drive.

*There is an excellent view of the largest of the ornate pools landscaped into the grounds of Fairlawne, a product of the 18th-century fashion for reshaping natural features into more aesthetically-pleasing designs.*

- Turn left along the drive, and almost immediately take a right fork, passing a bridge and buildings on your right. Keep straight on past the buildings where the drive ends, to a small wooden gate standing beside a field gate.
- Go through the gate and straight on along a path, passing occasional prominent trees just to the right of you. Pass between immature trees to reach a footbridge over a river.
- Cross the bridge and proceed half-right up the field, aiming for the corner of a protruding hedge seen ahead.
- Go through a stile in the field corner and along an enclosed footpath.
- On reaching a drive, keep straight on to Shipbourne village green, in front of the Village Hall and on the edge of an expanse of common.
- Bear left down the side of the green, keeping houses on your left, to converge with the main road in 100 yards.
- Turn left along the main road, but in 10 yards turn left down a footpath at a concrete marker, to the right of a white house and just to the left of No.1 New Cottage.
- Pass between a hedge and a garage to enter a field.
- Keep straight on down the right-hand edge of the field.
- Where the hedge on the right swings away, keep straight on across the field, aiming for an obvious track going up the slope ahead.

- Ascend the track, passing the buildings of Fairlawne Home Farm on your left.
- Keep straight on past the farm buildings on your left and keeping a large field to your right, to go onto a farm access road.
- Follow the access road down to a lane.
- Cross the lane to a stile immediately opposite and go straight on across the field, aiming for a stile visible in the middle of the wood directly ahead.
- Cross the stile into the wood and take the left fork of the path. Follow the path through woods to a field.
- Go half-right across the shoulder of the field, aiming for the roof of a building that soon comes into sight. Continue to a stile that is soon seen ahead.
- Cross the stile and keep on down the right-hand side of a small paddock, to a kissing gate leading onto a lane.
- Turn left along the lane for 100 yards to reach the Kentish Volunteer public house.
- Follow Roughouse Lane in front of the Kentish Volunteer for a quarter of a mile, to cross a small stream at a road bridge.
- Continue along the lane as it climbs uphill, swinging left and then right.
- Nearly at the summit of the hill, and immediately before the prominent Roughway Farm, turn left onto a footpath leading into some orchards.
- Keep the buildings of the farm on your right and pass around the right-hand edge of two small orchards.
- Cross a cross track and continue straight on, with orchards to your left and a high hedge to your right. Continue along the track, ignoring side turnings, for nearly a quarter of a mile, until a metal field gate is reached.
- Go through the gate and onto an enclosed track. Turn left and follow the track down to a country lane.
- Turn right along Old Soar Lane for a third of a mile to reach Old Soar Manor.

*Old Soar Manor House was built in 1290 and is one of the finest examples of a fortified knights house in England. It was built by the Culpepper family, who were the lords of the manor of Plaxtol and lived there until 1600.*

*There was no village at Plaxtol in 1290. The manor consisted of scattered farms built along the only two proper roads through the forest and isolated peasants dwellings, little more than hovels, in the forest. The nearest settlement of any size was Wrotham, five miles away along narrow and isolated roads through the forest. Although Wrotham was a sizeable settlement, with an Archbishop's court, it was a two or three-hour hazardous journey away.*

*Old Soar Manor House is stoutly built of Kentish ragstone and easily defensible against banditry. Access was by only one small and solid door leading into the undercroft, a large room into which livestock and movable possessions could be gathered quickly in an emergency. The slit windows had cross-loops from which the defender could easily train a cross bow to cover all approaches to the house.*

*The main living quarters were on the first floor, with a great hall for the communal living of the time and a chapel. The only access to the first floor was up one narrow spiral staircase. Should intruders manage to gain access to the ground floor, they would still have to fight their way up the staircase. This is of the standard mediaeval design, spiralling in a clockwise direction and therefore giving the advantage to a defender retreating up the stairs while wielding a sword in his right hand. Finally, there was a door of solid local oak at the top of the stairway, the final defence against intruders.*

*Old Soar could not have withstood a serious assault or a siege, but was ideal for withstanding the hit and run raids of casual bandits.*

**Old Soar Manor is open from April to September, 10am–6pm daily and entry is free.**

- After looking at Old Soar Manor, retrace your steps down Old Soar Lane for 150 yards, passing cottages on your left, to reach a dip in the road at a stream. Here turn right onto a signposted footpath.
- Follow the right bank of a small stream, at first along a broad track. Where this track swings away to the right, keep straight on along a narrow and vague footpath, keeping the stream to your left.
- Continue to follow the stream around to the left, on a path which soon becomes clearer, until a field is reached.
- Keep straight on along the left-hand edge of the field. At the bottom of the field, ignore a stile on the left, but five yards further on cross a wooden footbridge.
- Keep straight on up the path to reach a lane. Turn left and follow the lane into the outskirts of Plaxtol.
- Bear right with the road, walking up The Street. Keep going up the bill, passing residential side turnings and eventually passing the Papermakers Arms.
- Continue up the road to a T-junction, where you turn right back to the church.

A Georgian extension onto the Old Soar Manor House.

WALK 12

# Leeds Castle: fortresses and prisons in the Middle Ages

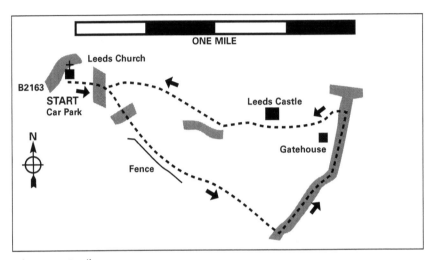

**Distance:** 2.5 miles

**Map:** OS sheet 188

**Start and Parking:** The walk commences at Leeds Church (grid ref: 826533), at the north end of Leeds village. Leeds is on the B2163, one mile south of the A20, and three miles east of Maidstone. There is a car park at the church itself.

**Refreshments:** Public house in Leeds. Tearoom in Leeds Castle.

### Historical Background

The original castle at Leeds was Saxon, built in 857 by Ledian, chief minister to King Ethelbert. After the Norman Conquest it was given to the Crevecour family, who enlarged the castle substantially. During the Barons' rebellion of 1258–65, Robert Crevecour originally supported the King, but changed allegiances just in time to be on the losing side and so was dispossessed by Henry III. Leeds Castle officially became a royal castle during the reign of Edward I.

Edward II appointed Lord Badlemere as 'castellan', a royal officer who held a castle on behalf of his sovereign. It was during this period that Leeds saw its only military activity. In 1321 Edward's wife, Queen Isabella, on pilgrimage to Canterbury, decided to stay at Leeds. Lady Badlemere, in charge of the castle during her husband's absence and fiercely hostile towards the Queen, barred the gates and refused Isabella entry. In the ensuing argument her men killed six of the Queen's retinue. In the heated climate of factional in-fighting that surrounded Edward's court at this time, insults were heaped onto injury until the king himself led a small army, predominantly of Londoners, to besiege Leeds Castle. The castle fell after a few days fierce fighting, its 'seneschal' (chief military officer) Walter Colepepper was hung and Lady Badlemere was confined to the Tower of London.

Leeds Castle was a royal possession for a further two centuries, during which time it saw service mainly as a prison. Richard II was briefly imprisoned here after his deposition by Henry IV. Henry IV imprisoned his queen, Mary de Bohun, here for supporting her sons in their dispute with their father in his later years. Eleanor of Gloucester was tried for witchcraft in Leeds in 1431 in an attempt to discredit her husband, the powerful Lord Protector Duke Humphrey, and spent the rest of her life imprisoned here. During the 17th century, French and Dutch prisoners of war were confined in Leeds Castle.

Henry VIII gave the castle to Sir Anthony St Leger as a reward for services rendered, and thereafter the castle passed into the hands of various private landowners, including the Colepepper family, whose ancestor had been executed for doing his duty defending the castle.

## The Walk
**This short walk crosses the parkland around Leeds Castle and the quiet lanes and fields nearby, as well as passing under the walls of the castle itself.**

● Leave the car park and turn right to enter the churchyard.

*The Church of St Nicholas is Saxon in origin, with the typical high narrow nave of Saxon churches and two Anglo-Saxon windows on the north wall. The tower is a Norman addition and there is a fine rood screen from the slightly later Perpendicular period of architecture.*

● Pass through the churchyard, passing the church on your left and keeping to the right-hand fence, to exit via a kissing gate at the bottom of the churchyard.
● Cross the field, aiming for the left side of a hedge seen opposite. Follow the hedge on your right hand to a gate into a lane.
● Cross the lane and go through a kissing gate into a field.
● Go half-right aiming for a stile on the far side of the field, between two tall trees.
● Cross the stile and keep ahead, crossing a drive and passing to the left of a clump of mature trees 50 yards ahead, aiming for the corner of a fence beyond.
● At the corner of the fence, keep ahead, with the fence close on your right.
● Once the field corner is reached, pass through a field gate and bear half-right to pick up a path through trees. Continue along the same line of advance along a path.
● Leave the plantation and keep straight on along an enclosed footpath.
● When the path meets a cross track, turn left down the track and follow it out to a lane.

- Turn left down the lane. Pass a post box and then some cottages on your right and follow the lane to cross a stream.

*This stream is the River Len, whose waters were diverted to provide the artificial lake now surrounding Leeds Castle.*

- Go along the lane for nearly another half mile, climbing steadily up a hill and then descending the other side.
- Pass the private entrance to Leeds Castle on your left, and after a further 50 yards turn left through a gate and descend some steps to a golf course.
- At the bottom of the steps leave the path and turn left, following the field boundary around to reach a drive.
- Turn right along the drive. Ignore a turn to the left in 200 yards but keep straight on towards the castle.

*The original Saxon castle was reasonably large by the standards of the ninth century, but nowhere near the size seen today. It originally stood on dry ground, without the lake we see now. The first enlargements were made by the original Norman owners, the Crevecour family, who initially constructed a motte and bailey, an earthen mound surrounded by a simple wooden palisade. The Crevecours soon replaced the wooden stockade with a stone curtain wall, and then substantially enlarged the keep in 1119 (seen today on the innermost of the islands upon which the castle stands).*

*Two hundred years later, during the reign of Edward I, the de Leybourne family strengthened the fortifications in line with the new military technology imported into*

Leeds Castle, dating from Norman times, has been considerably altered and extended over the centuries.

*Britain by the king and built the stone curtain wall, turrets and gatehouse we see today. They also surrounded the castle with a dry moat, crossed by a drawbridge, and protected this by increasing the strength of the gatehouse and building a Barbican or gatehouse at the outer end of the drawbridge.*

*In the 17th century the castle was under the charge of Sir John Evelyn, who flooded the dry moat by diverting the River Len, built a new drawbridge between the two mounds, now islands, brought fresh spring water into the castle, and created the artificial lake seen today.*

*In the 19th century Leeds Castle passed to the Wykeham–Martin family, who built a range of mock-tudor buildings on the central island. Much of the 'mediaeval' building seen today is in fact a 19th-century folly, although some of the 13th-century fortifications can still be seen.*

The castle is privately owned and often used as a conference centre. It is open to the public on occasions and contains an impressive collection of paintings and furnishings, and a pair of Anne Boleyn's shoes. There is an admission charge for the castle but with public rights of way across the grounds.

● Cross between the moat and the lake to the castle entrance. Turn right opposite the bridge.

*On the right is a fortified mill. The mill was an important part of a mediaeval castle, producing flour for the lord and his retainers, and a channel from the River Len provided the motive power for the mill wheel. This fortified mill was built in 1300, connected by a covered way and fortified walls to the Barbican, with iron gates over the millstream to prevent access. It was constructed in order to provide a continued source of flour even during siege conditions.*

● Follow the drive. Do not turn right at an exit sign but keep straight on, keeping the lake on your left and climbing the drive.
● Pass through a gate beside a cattle grid and bear right across the grassy slope, keeping the drive just to your left and aiming for a marker post just to the right of where the drive turns left.
● At the marker post, keep ahead up the grassy slope, maintaining the same line of advance and leaving the drive behind you. Aim just to the left of a stand of trees seen ahead. Two marker posts lead you to a kissing gate.

*There are fine views back from this point across the parkland, formally landscaped in the 18th century by Capability Brown, to the castle.*

● Keep straight on along the bottom of a field, with the field boundary on your right hand side, to reach a gate in the fence on the opposite side.
● Cross the next field, keeping to the right-hand edge, and pass into a lane.
● Cross the lane, enter the field and keep ahead with the field boundary on your left. Where the hedge bends left, keep straight on to a gate into the churchyard.
● Pass through the churchyard and back to the car park.

WALK 13

# Ightham Mote: from Plantagenet stronghold to Tudor home

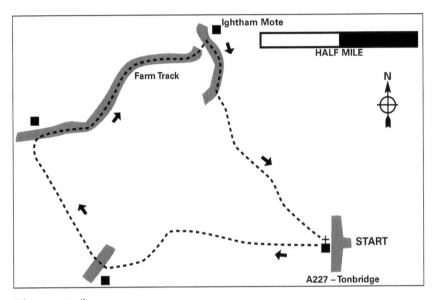

**Distance:** 4 miles

**Map:** OS sheet 188

**Start and Parking:** The walk starts from Shipbourne Church (grid ref: 591523). There is free parking on Shipbourne Common, opposite the church. Shipbourne itself is on the A227, three miles north on Tonbridge.

**Refreshments:** Public house at Shipbourne

### Historical Background

Ightham Mote is two miles south of Ightham village, one of the oldest and prettiest villages in Kent. It dates from Saxon times and took its peculiar name from the Saxon king Ehta or Ohta and the Saxon word 'ham' or homestead. The house stands on the spot where the Saxon council, or Moot, used to meet, and the name of the house probably derives from this, rather than the fact that it is moated.

The house itself was built over a period of three centuries. It was started in 1340 as a fortified home by the Cawne family, loyal supporters of the Plantagenets who were rewarded for their services by grants of land in Kent. In the middle of the 14th century Kent was still heavily forested in many places, with poor communications and widely-spaced settlements, and the rich and wealthy had to look to their own protection. In consequence, Sir Thomas Cawne built his home with high strong walls and small, easily-protected windows, and surrounded it with a wide moat.

With time the countryside of Kent became less wild. More and more villages surrounded by rich agricultural land grew up, the forests receded, roads improved and the county became far less lawless. This was reflected by changes in Ightham Mote, where the emphasis shifted from construction for defence to building for comfort.

Although the moat remained and crenellations were added in Tudor times, their purpose was largely for decoration. From the 17th century onwards, Ightham was the family home for rich London merchants, whose property might be threatened by burglary but no longer needed the house's impressive defences.

### The Walk

**This walk starts at Shipbourne and goes through rolling arable land, still with a hint of the forests that used to cover the area. It then climbs along the Greensand Ridge to Ightham before returning through woods and fields to Shipbourne.**

- Enter the churchyard via the lychgate and follow the path around the church, keeping the church to your left. At the rear of the church, leave the churchyard via a kissing gate.
- Ignore a stile immediately on the right, but instead keep straight on down the side of the field, with a fence on the right.
- Leave the field through a large gap in the hedge. Bear quarter-right across the large field in front. Aim for the right-hand corner of the wood seen ahead, protruding into the field.
- At the corner of the wood, cross a stile and enter the trees. Follow the footpath straight on as it winds through the trees, with the boundary of the field parallel to the path on the right.
- Where the field on the right ends, climb with the path to join a crossing track. Turn right for 10 yards, then turn left onto a footpath, climbing through trees.
- After 100 yards, where the path levels out, ignore a path to the right but instead keep straight on along a broad grassy track.
- Follow the track, soon with a fence on your left, as it winds gently downhill through trees, ignoring all turnings to the right and left.
- The track becomes fenced on both sides and drops towards a cottage seen ahead. Upon reaching the cottage (Budds Oast), turn right to reach a road.
- Turn right along the road for 15 yards, then turn left across a stile by a field gate.
- Once over the stile, immediately turn right through a gap in the hedge, then immediately turn left again. Walk down the side of the field, with your back to the road and the hedge on your left.
- Where the hedge turns left at a prominent tree, continue half-right across the field, making for the edge of a wood ahead.

- At the edge of the wood, go through a gap in the hedge and cross a footbridge.
- Continue straight on across the field, aiming for the edge of some trees seen 100 yards ahead.
- On reaching the trees continue straight on up the field edge, with the field on your right and trees on your left.
- At the top of the field cross a stile. Continue straight up the field, aiming for a stile just to the left of a house seen ahead.
- Cross the stile and turn right into a metalled drive.
- Follow the track for a mile, crossing over a cross track after half a mile.
- The track eventually reaches Mote Farm. Pass through the farm outbuildings to a road and turn right past the entrance to Ightham Mote.

*Ightham Mote is a late mediaeval building, extensively remodelled in Tudor times and lived in for the past 600 years. Built of oak and local ragstone, Ightham Mote contains architectural gems from many periods.*

*The earliest part of the house was built in the middle of the 14th century by Sir Thomas Cawne, who fought in France with the Black Prince at the start of the Hundred Years War and who lived in Ightham from 1340 until his death in 1374. Of his building, the moat, the Great Hall, the Chapel and Solar all still remain as fine examples of the Decorated Period of architecture.*

*On Sir Thomas's death, the house passed to the Haute family, the most famous member of which, Sir Edward Haute, was a cousin of Elizabeth Woodville, Edward IV's queen, and who was appointed High Sheriff of Kent in 1478. He built the Gate Tower and squared off the west and south wings. Haute was party to the attempts by the Woodvilles to keep Richard of Gloucester, later Richard III, from power. When Edward IV died in April 1483 it was his*

The moated Tudor manor house of Ightham Mote.

*wish that his brother, Richard of Gloucester, should be Lord Protector of England, to avoid the factional in-fighting that seemed likely. Haute was part of the group that tried to hurry the young Prince Edward (later Edward V) to London and crown him before his fathers wish could be carried out. This was frustrated by the prompt action of Richard. Vaughan, Rivers and Grey, leaders of the Woodville clan, were executed for this act. Haute escaped this fate but later that same year he joined the Duke of Buckingham in his revolt against Richard, for which he was condemned and his lands confiscated. Haute was later pardoned by Henry VII.*

*In 1521 a minor Tudor courtier, Sir Richard Clement, bought the house and extensively remodelled it. The Tudor Chapel dates from 1521 and contains a magnificent painted ceiling and glass with coats of arms, including the Tudor Rose and the pomegranate, symbol of Katherine of Aragon, as signs of the family's loyal support for the ruling house. Clement also added the Oriel Room, remodelled the courtyard, and crenellated the outer walls, more for artistic fancy than for any need for defence. A later Clement married Lady Dorothy Selby, a lady-in-waiting to Queen Elizabeth I.*

*In 1637 the house passed from the Clement family to Dorothy Selby and her family, affluent London merchants and powerful figures in the local politics of Kent rather than players on the national political scene. The Selbys continued to add to and remodel the house: the Oriel room contains a fine Jacobean fireplace, while the drawing room has a Palladian window from the 18th century.*

**The Mote is owned by the National Trust and is open from mid-March to the end of October, 10.30am–5.30pm daily, apart from Tuesdays and Saturdays.**

- One hundred yards past the entrance to Ightham Mote, cross a stile on the left and follow the right-hand edge of the field to a stile.
- Cross the stile and bear left across a small field to cross a stile into woods.
- Follow the track with a fence on your left through conifers. Ignore a cross track and follow the track to reach a stile into a field.
- Go straight across the field. At the far side, turn left and follow the hedge down and around to the right, to the bottom of the field.
- At the bottom of the field, cross a track to a stile opposite.
- Cross the stile and head half-right across the field, aiming just to the right of a plantation of trees seen ahead.
- Keep the plantation on your left side and continue up the field to a stile.
- Cross the stile and continue to a second stile five yards ahead, leading into the corner of a field.
- Go up the left side of the field, aiming towards the church. Cross a tarmacked drive and keep straight on towards a stile seen ahead, recrossing the drive in the process.
- Turn left to the kissing gate back into Shipbourne churchyard.

*Shipbourne Church was rebuilt in 1723 on the site of an older mediaeval church. It contains a fine monument to local landlord Lord Barnard.*

WALK 14
# Knole House and Jack Cade's revolt 1450

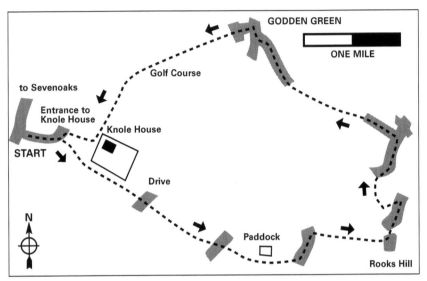

**Distance:** 6 miles

**Map:** OS sheet 188

**Start and Parking:** The walk starts at the main gates to Knole Park (grid ref: 534543), located at the southern end of Sevenoaks High Street and clearly signposted from the town. There is ample parking in Sevenoaks itself, both in car parks and on the road.

**Refreshments:** Shops, pubs and tearooms in Sevenoaks; tearoom at Knole House when open; pub at Godden Green.

## Historical Background

By the 15th century Kent was enjoying a period of major economic prosperity. Its proximity to Europe meant that its ports and its inland market towns benefitted from the increasing trade with the Continent. The growing population in nearby London meant ever-bigger markets for its rich agricultural lands. It had a buoyant textile trade based on wool, with both London and the Continent.

However, by the middle of the century the people of Kent perceived their prosperity to be threatened. The loss of France at the end of the Hundred Years War and the resulting closure of continental markets was blamed on the incompetence of royal advisers during Henry VI's minority. Londoners were perceived to have received licence to poach on the preserves of

Kentish merchants. The textile trade was threatened by the influx of Flemish refugees who offered cheap and efficient competition. On top of all this, there was widespread corruption by royal and county officials, who controlled the courts and parliament and thus stifled any legitimate route of protest. One of the chief offenders was Lord Saye & Sale, Lord Lieutenant of Kent and owner of Knole House and Hever Castle (see walk 15).

This deepening sense of grievance erupted in 1450. A series of spontaneous revolts broke out among the people of Kent, not among the peasantry but among people of substance who were protesting about their loss of prosperity and influence. These protests were soon pulled together into one movement, led by Jack Cade, a gentleman soldier of fortune with ambiguous political ambitions. Cade imposed a reasonable military discipline on his followers, assembled a vast following in Ashford and marched on London. At Sevenoaks he defeated a royal army sent to oppose him. He was welcomed into London by its populace, and there the rebels executed Lord Saye & Sale. Henry VI acceded to the rebels demands, then went back on his word, and the rebellion foundered. Cade died while fleeing for safety.

**The Walk**
**This walk goes through Knole Park, near the site of one of Jack Cade's victories. It then crosses the attractive Greensand landscape to Godden Green before returning through woodland to Knole House.**

- Enter Knole Park via the main gates and proceed up the drive. After 100 yards, bear right off the main drive up a tarmacked footpath.
- Where the footpath forks, bear right and continue uphill.
- As Knole House comes into sight ahead, bear off half-right from the tarmacked path, at a 'Greensand Link Path' sign, and proceed around and up the hillside, aiming for the right-hand corner of the wall that surrounds the grounds of the house.

*Just off to the right of the path is a brick dome. This is the roof of an Ice House. Before modern day refrigeration techniques, the storage of meats all year around was extremely difficult. Up until the early Middle Ages, meat could either be eaten almost as soon as it was killed, or heavily preserved with salt. This made the diet increasingly unpalatable as the winter months progressed. An ingenious solution was the ice house, a deep brick-lined cylinder dug into the earth and roofed. In the winter months, blocks of ice would be cut and placed in the cylinder, which was straw lined to keep the temperature stable. If the ice house was correctly designed, a supply of slowly melting ice would remain available until the following winter, enabling meat to be preserved fresh throughout the year.*

- Turn around the corner of the wall.

*Pause just after turning the corner and look to your right across the valley, to the church seen through the trees on the opposite side. That point, just outside the boundary of Knole Park, was where Jack Cade's rebels defeated the royal army. The king's military advisers were*

*guilty of complacence and arrogance in dealing with the rebellion. They assumed that because they were soldiers and gentlemen and their opponents commoners and rebels, that it would be an easy task to crush the rebel force. In this, they totally underestimated the military skill of Cade, himself a professional soldier who had, in remarkably short time, forged his men into an efficient and disciplined fighting force. They also totally overestimated their own abilities as soldiers. The royal army was routed in a battle lasting less than an hour, and Cade's men marched on towards London, where they lured a second royal force into ambush and defeat at Eltham.*

- Continue with the wall on your left for one complete side of the walled grounds.

*The walls were built for both privacy and defence. They would not withstand determined assault but, with the memory of Jack Cade's rebellion still fresh in the builder's mind, are high enough to keep out casual bandits or marauders.*

- Where the wall turns a corner, keep straight on across the park, following a rough track.
- One hundred and fifty yards after leaving the wall, turn right with the track into trees and bracken. Pass around a fallen tree (blown down in the hurricane of 1987) and 40 yards later cross a track and continue straight on down a tarmacked path.
- After 800 yards cross over a driveway and continue straight on, now on a grassy path. Walk alongside a deer fence to a gate leading onto the road.

The Tudor mansion of Knole House, standing in 1,000 acres of parkland.

- Cross the road and follow a footpath into the woods. Follow the footpath as it winds through trees to a stile leading into a paddock.
- Cross the stile and turn right, following the right-hand edge of the paddock around two sides of the field, to exit in the bottom right-hand corner over a somewhat concealed stile.
- Descend and cross over a track to a stile opposite.
- Cross the stile and follow an enclosed footpath for 500 yards along the top of a field, past a tennis court and fenced grounds. Eventually reach the road at the entrance to a house.
- Turn left up the road. After 100 yards turn right up a footpath, signposted Greensand Way.
- Climb steadily up through trees, staying to the main path and ignoring side turnings. After 400 yards cross an open area with a bench to your left and continue straight on into trees again.
- Two hundred yards later, turn right at a T-junction of paths.
- At a fork in 50 yards, stay to the right, and 30 yards later turn right with the path and descend to enter a wood.
- Follow the path as it winds down through trees, with steep drops and intermittent wide views to the right. Eventually descend with the path down some steps to the driveway of a house at Rooks Hill.
- Turn left at the bottom of the steps and go steeply up a track through trees.

- At the top of the slope, bear right along a tarmacked drive, passing houses on your left. 150 yards past the last house, turn sharp left onto a bridleway.
- At a T-junction of paths, turn left.
- Continue along the path for 150 yards, then turn right downhill for 20 yards to join another path at a T-junction. Here turn right again.
- Descend this wider path through trees and bracken. At a junction of paths in 300 yards turn right.
- Follow the path for a further 300 yards to reach a road. Turn right and follow the road as it climbs, passing houses on the left.
- Just before reaching a crossroads, turn left up a driveway, at a concrete footpath sign and with a post bearing a dozen house names.
- Go down the drive for 400 yards. You initially have houses to your left and a hedge to your right, then paddocks to the left and cottages to the right. Where the drive turns into the gates of a house called 'Cherry Trees', keep straight on down an enclosed footpath.
- Ignore a path off to the left apparently leading to a tennis court, but keep straight on to a stile.
- Cross the stile and keep straight on across a field, aiming for the end of a band of trees seen ahead. Continue uphill, keeping to the left-hand side of the field.
- Continue straight on through a band of trees. Where the trees end, keep straight on, aiming for a stile into woods on the opposite side of the field. You will need to curve slightly right around a clump of trees ahead in order to maintain your forward direction.

The gatehouse of Knole house.

- Cross the stile and continue up into the woods. Keep straight on, crossing over two cross tracks.
- The path eventually emerges onto an unmade drive. Keep straight on up the drive. You soon join a tarmacked lane at the gates of Godden Clink, where you continue straight on to reach a road.
- Turn right up the road. 30 yards past the Bucks Head public house, turn left at a concrete footpath marker.
- Keep straight on along an unmade track for 100 yards to reach a lane. Cross the lane to a footpath opposite leading to a swing gate into woods.
- Follow the path into the woods. After 100 yards, bear left at a T-junction, onto a sandy track.
- Follow the track to a gate and kissing gate. Pass through the kissing gate into Knole Park.

*Knole House is visible off to your left, and Sevenoaks soon becomes visible to the right. Sevenoaks is now largely a dormitory for London. It was named in AD1100 from the seven oak trees that stood nearby, and traditionally seven oaks have been maintained in the town ever since. Six of the seven oaks that were ceremoniously planted to commemorate the coronation of Edward VII in 1901 were blown down in the great storm of 1987, and six new ones were replanted the following year.*

*The park itself covers 1,000 acres, and is six miles in circumference. There is an extensive deer herd roaming the park, access to which is free to walkers. Deer had once freely grazed the forests of Kent, but by the end of the 15th century increasing agricultural use and the heavy demand for wood to provide charcoal had resulted in the forest shrinking dramatically. Increasingly, great landowners would enclose large swathes of land and stock them with their own deer herds, especially bred and managed to provide hunting for the landowner and his guests.*

- Follow the track, now metalled, as it descends into the park and crosses a golf course, before climbing to reach Knole House.
- On reaching the house, turn right to reach the main entrance.

*Knole House was originally a small manor house until it and its surrounding parkland were bought by Lord Saye & Sale, who extended it to create a country home suitable for a leading courtier. The death of Lord Saye & Sale during Jack Cade's rebellion put Knole Park and manor house on the market, in a climate where property prices in Kent were depressed. Thomas Bouchier, Archbishop of Canterbury, bought Knole in 1455 for the knockdown price of £256, and he set about redesigning the house to transform it into a palace fit for a prince of the church. It remained an ecclesiastical palace until the 1530s, when Henry VIII dropped heavy hints to Archbishop Cranmer that he would like Knole as a royal palace (the same tactic Henry had previously used upon Cardinal Wolsey to acquire Hampton Court).*

*It remained in the hands of the Crown until 1566, when Elizabeth I gave Knole to her cousin Thomas Sackville, first Earl of Dorset. Sackville considerably extended the house to basically its current shape. Sackville was both a poet and a diplomat and the house has stayed in the family ever since. A descendant of the first Earl was the poet Vita Sackville-West, whose friend Virginia Woolf describes Knole in her novel* Orlando.

*Knole is one of the largest private houses in England. Architecturally it is one of the finest and certainly one of the largest Tudor houses in England. Its roofs cover four acres. An intriguing feature is the link of its design to the calendar: it contains 365 rooms, one for each day of the year, 52 staircases, one for each week, seven courtyards, one for each day of the week, and 12 entrances, one for each month.*

*Although the basic outline of the house remains as it was laid down in the time of Henry VIII, it has been added to and altered over the centuries by the Sackvilles and today contains a fascinating mixture of architectural developments: its two gatehouses are largely unchanged since Archbishop Bouchier's day, the Great Hall is Tudor and has a magnificent carved-oak screen, the great staircase and associated galleries date from the Stuart era, while many of the bedrooms leading off the galleries remain as they were redeveloped in Georgian times, with four-poster beds in all the major bedrooms.*

*The family still live in part of the house, while the rest is administered by the National Trust. It contains a fine collection of paintings, tapestries and furnishings, combining a history of the Sackville family with a history of English furniture and textile design.*

**It is open from Easter to the end of October, Wednesday to Saturday, 12 noon–4pm. There is an admission charge, but it is free to National Trust members.**

● On leaving the house, go directly away from the front door down the driveway opposite. At a T-junction take the footpath opposite and follow it downhill to reach the drive back to the main gates.

## WALK 15
# Hever Castle and two Tudor queens

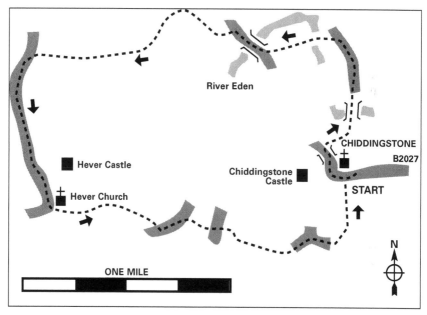

**Distance:** 5 miles

**Map:** OS sheet 188

**Start and Parking:** The walk starts from the church at Chiddingstone (grid ref: 501452). Chiddingstone is on a minor road one mile south of Bough Beech, which is itself on the B2027 between Limpfield and Tonbridge. There is limited parking in the village of Chiddingstone. As an alternative, the walk could be started from Hever.

**Refreshments:** Public house and tearooms in Chiddingstone and a public house in Hever.

### Historical Background

Hever Castle has close connections with two of the wives of Henry VIII. In 1527 England was facing a dynastic crisis. For nearly a century the smooth succession of the Crown had been disputed, by Civil War, rebellion and factional in-fighting. The major obsession of Henry VIII was to ensure that the Crown would pass without dispute to his heir. This meant a son, for it was feared that any woman would see her claim contested and Civil War would be unleashed again.

But Henry's happy marriage to Katherine of Aragon for 20 years had produced only a daughter, Mary, and a string of still-births. Dynastic demands, and maybe his own deeply-held religious beliefs as well, led Henry to put aside Katherine in favour of the vivacious and intelligent Anne, daughter of Sir Thomas Bullen of Hever.

Forcing through a divorce from Queen Katherine required Henry to take the extreme step of breaking with the Church of Rome and being excommunicated, and his second marriage to Anne raised disquiet among many of his nobles due to her perceived lowly origins. To cap it all, Henry's dynastic plans were thwarted when Anne only succeeded in giving birth to another daughter, Elizabeth. A second divorce was seen as impossible, and trumped-up charges of adultery and incest were needed to dispose of Anne, who was beheaded in 1536. Sir Thomas Bullen left court under a cloud and died at Hever in 1538. His estates passed to the Crown.

Henry's third wife Jane Seymour gave him the son he needed so desperately, but Jane died during childbirth. In 1540 Henry married for a fourth time, this time for purely diplomatic reasons.

In order to cement an alliance with Protestant northern Europe, he married Anne, daughter of the Duke of Cleves. The marriage was never consummated and divorce followed shortly after. Anne co-operated fully with Henry's decisions and was rewarded with a generous pension and several properties, including the Hever estates of her predecessor.

### The Walk

**This walk starts in the Tudor village of Chiddingstone, with its mock-mediaeval castle, and goes through the peaceful Eden Valley to Hever. Here it passes Hever Castle and Hever Church, burial place of Sir Thomas Bullen, before returning through Greensand landscape.**

● Standing in the main street of Chiddingstone, with the houses and shops on your left and the church on your right, walk down the road, bearing right around the church.

*Chiddingstone is a perfectly preserved mediaeval and Tudor village. The house that is now the village post office and shop dates from 1453. Other houses bear such dates as 1638 and 1643, presumably the dates of subsequent alterations since the deeds of the houses show them to be much older, and their half-timbered construction and overhanging first floors argue for an earlier construction. The houses were mainly built by local farmers and tradesmen and reflect the affluence of the village. At the end of the street are wrought-iron gates leading into Chiddingstone Castle. Originally, the main street of the village passed through these gates and ran through the castle grounds, but the road was diverted in the late 18th century by the castle owners, to give themselves more privacy*

*The village takes its name from Chiding Stone, an ancient sarsen stone that was used in mediaeval times as a pulpit at which those who had offended against the code of conduct of the village would have their misdemeanours listed and would be punished by their neighbours. The original chiding stone is in the garden of the houses opposite the church.*

*The Church of St Mary was largely rebuilt after a fire in 1624, although the tower and its rude gargoyles are 15th century and the lower part of the nave arcades and some of the windows are from the 14th century. Inside the church are grave slabs made of iron, a reminder of the former Wealdan iron industry upon which much of the wealth of the area is based. The earliest grave slab dates from 1601, for Richard Streatfeild, ironmaster. In the churchyard is the mausoleum of the Streatfeild family, owners of Chiddingstone Castle. It contains over 60 coffins and is ventilated via a false altar tomb nearby.*

- One hundred yards past the church, the road crosses a bridge. There are views of Chiddingstone Castle across the lake to the left.

*Richard Streatfeild made his fortune out of the local iron industry during the first Industrial Revolution (see also walk 17) and settled in a Tudor manor house where Chiddingstone Castle now stands. A later Streatfeild replaced the Tudor building with a fashionable brick house called High Street House, around 1680. At the beginning of the 19th century Henry Streatfeild fancied himself as a feudal lord of the manor and turned the house into a mock-mediaeval castle by adding battlements and turrets and digging an artificial lake. He then high-handedly diverted the village street away from his property and demolished a few cottages that spoilt his view. The building was completed by Henry's son in 1835 and stayed in the family until the last Streatfeild died in 1938.*

Chiddingstone Castle contains Tudor panelling and 16th-century stained glass, as well as Jacobite relics and a collection of Oriental Objects D'art.

- Immediately after crossing the bridge, turn right through a metal swing gate and walk down the right-hand side of a field.
- At the bottom of the field turn right through a gap in the hedge and follow the path half-left across the field, aiming at a stile at the left corner of the wood seen ahead.
- Cross the stile onto a metalled footpath and turn left. Follow the footpath between fields to a footbridge over a river.
- Cross the footbridge and continue straight on along an enclosed footpath to reach a gate onto a driveway.
- Keep straight on along the driveway, passing cottages on the right. Bear left with the drive, passing Rectory Cottage on the left and, 250 yards later, North Cottage on the right.
- Twenty yards past North Cottage, cross a stile on the left. Walk straight across the field (the path may not always be in evidence) and down to a metal-railed footbridge across the River Eden.

*On the left is a brick pillbox built during World War Two to command the River Eden. In 1940–41 there was a real threat of a German invasion, and successive lines of defence were built along all natural features, from the channel coast right up to London. These were designed to contest an enemy's advance at every stage.*

- Cross the bridge and continue straight on across the next big field. Again, the path may not be evident, but aim for a gate visible on the far side and almost directly in front of you.
- Cross a stile by the gate and turn right along the road, again crossing the Eden.

*Another of the pillboxes defending the Eden crossing is seen on the left.*

- Continue along the road for 150 yards, then turn left across a stile by a gate.
- Continue straight on up the left-hand edge of the field for 100 yards, then turn left through a gap in the hedge. Immediately turn right and, continuing the line of advance, go on up the right-hand edge of the field.
- After 300 yards, at the top of the slope, bear right through a field gate. Still continue the former line of advance, now on the left-hand side of a field.
- Just past a barn and field gate, turn left down an enclosed path to cross a stile onto a track.
- Turn right along the track for 10 yards, then cross a second track to a stile into a field.
- Turn left along the left-hand edge of the field.
- At the bottom of the field cross a stile into the golf course.
- Turn left for 20 yards to reach a wooden shelter, then continue straight on down the track to cross the fairway.
- Follow the track across a bridge, and 20 yards later go straight on across a cross track. Go through a large gap in the hedge and up a broad tree-lined track, with a hedge on the right and trees and fairway on the left.
- Continue straight along the track for half a mile, in between fairways and with a half-timbered building visible off to the right. Ignore all cross tracks and side turns.
- Where the track turns right to the clubhouse, keep straight on across a stile and along an enclosed footpath. Follow the path for 200 yards to reach the road.
- Turn left along the road. After a quarter of a mile Hever Castle can be glimpsed across the fence to your left.
- Cross the bridge with the road and continue for a further 100 yards to reach Hever Castle.

*Hever Castle started as a fortified manor house, with moat, drawbridge and portcullis (it contains the only working wooden portcullis left in England) and was built by Walter de Hevere around 1340. The manor was rarely used as a home, but passed through a number of distinguished owners in the next hundred years, including Sir John Fastolf (immortalised as Falstaff by Shakespeare) and Lord Saye & Sale, the unpopular Lord Lieutenant of Kent who also owned Knole House and was beheaded by Jack Code's rebels (see walk 14).*

*In 1462 it was bought by Sir Geoffrey Bullen, a Norfolk yeoman and businessman who rose to become Lord Mayor of London. Sir Geoffrey married into society, one of the very few means of advancement for families of non-noble birth. Geoffrey's son William improved the family fortunes still further by marrying a daughter of the Earl of Osmonde. William's son Thomas cemented the family's place by marrying the daughter of the powerful Thomas Howard, Duke of Norfolk. Thomas's daughter Anne married the king.*

Hever Castle, home to both Anne Boleyn and Anne of Cleaves.

*After the fall of Anne Boleyn (she changed the spelling of her name to a more fashionable version), Hever passed to Anne of Cleves. Anne was not the 'Flemish Mare' of legend, but was certainly plainer than her portraits had suggested and was also dull and straight-laced by the standards of the English court. She failed to attract Henry, who almost instantly decided upon another divorce. Anne shrewdly appealed to the romantic in Henry by asking for his help and guidance and was rewarded with a generous financial settlement, several palaces and the continued trappings of royalty. Anne lived for a further 17 years in happy retirement, much of it spent at Hever. On her death she was buried in Westminster Abbey, the only one of Henry's wives to achieve that honour.*

*After the death of Anne of Cleves, Hever eventually passed into private hands. During the 17th and 18th centuries it was used as a 'safe house' for smugglers bringing contraband up from Deal (see also walk 21) to meet wealthy customers who came down from London, with a percentage going to the owners of Hever. In 1903 it was bought by William Waldour Astor, an American millionaire who became the first Lord Astor and who renovated the house in a mock Tudor style. He also added the lake and a row of 'Tudor' cottages for effect.*

**The castle is now privately owned. It is open from March to November, 11am–5pm. There is an admission charge.**

- Pass the front entrance of Hever Castle to reach Hever Church.

*St Peter's Church was built in the 13th century in the Perpendicular style. It has an unusual shingle spire and a Jacobean pulpit. It also contains a fine 15th-century brass of Margaret Cheyne. Its main claim to fame is the side chapel to the Bullen Family, which contains a Tudor fireplace and chest, as well as a magnificent brass of Sir Thomas Bullen in the robes of the Order of the Garter. Thomas Bullen was a successful Diplomat in Henry VIII's foreign service, became treasurer to the Royal household in 1522 and was elevated to the peerage as Viscount Rochford in 1525. He introduced both his daughters, Mary and Anne, to court and both caught the attention of the king. Bullen was rewarded by becoming Earl of Wiltshire and Earl of Ormonde, before falling from favour after Anne's execution.*

- Enter the churchyard via the lychgate and take the footpath to the right of the church. Do not circle the church but keep straight on, to reach an enclosed footpath at the bottom of the churchyard.
- Descend the footpath, cross a footbridge and ascend between gardens and a field.
- Follow the enclosed footpath with the drive to Hever Castle on your left.

*Mock-mediaeval jousting takes palace in the meadow on the other side of the drive.*

- Follow the path as it leaves the drive and enters woodland.
- Cross the drive via a footbridge and continue until the path joins a drive.
- Continue along the grass verge until the drive is barred by a gate. Go through a smaller gate to the left, cross the drive and follow the path to the left of the cottage.
- Follow the path through a band of trees, with garden fences on the right, and down through scrubland, now with the hedge on the right.
- Cross a track, with houses close by on the left, and keep straight on along a footpath for 30 yards to reach a road.
- Cross the road and continue along an enclosed footpath. Follow the footpath to the right over a stile and along the left-hand edge of the field.

*Across the field to the right can be seen both round and square oast houses. The oast house is used for drying hops, part of the brewing industry which was for many years a stable part of the Kentish economy. Oast houses were originally square, but Kentish hop-growers decided that a round house would be more efficient, since it would not have any corners in which hops could collect and remain undried. Thus the round oast house, so associated with the image of Kent, came into being. With use, it was discovered that the round oast was no more efficient than the square one.*

- After 50 yards cross a footbridge on the left.
- Climb with the path through a wood and continue straight on where the slope levels out, to reach a stile into a field.

- Cross the stile and follow the enclosed path between deer fences around the left-hand edge of the field and into woods.
- Pass through a gully carved out of the Greensand and down through trees to join a track by a gate.
- Go through the gate and along the drive for 50 yards, then turn right up a sloping metalled track.
- At Hill Hoath Farm at the top of the slope, fork left into farm buildings. Pass a barn on the right and keep straight on along a footpath for 20 yards with a field fence on your left, to reach a stile by a gate.
- Cross the stile and keep straight on along the left-hand edge of the field and through a belt of trees to reach a stile on your left.
- Cross the stile and turn left to follow a footpath across the field. Chiddingstone Church soon becomes visible ahead.
- Cross a stile into an enclosed path and keep straight on for 175 yards, crossing a further stile en route, to reach a road at a kissing gate.
- Turn left back into Chiddingstone village.

WALK 16

# Penshurst: the growth of a Tudor palace

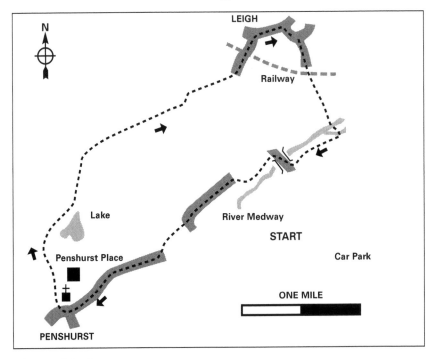

**Distance:** 5.5 miles

**Map:** OS sheet 188

**Start and Parking:** The walk starts from the village green at Leigh, on the B2027, four miles west of Tonbridge (grid ref: 550465). There is ample on-street parking in Leigh.

**Refreshments:** Public houses and shops in Leigh. Public house, shop and tearooms at Penshurst.

### Historical Background

Penshurst Place, like Knole House (walk 14), is more like a village than a single house, with wings added to existing buildings by successive generations of owners. Although of mediaeval origin, it flowered into one of the greatest privately-owned palaces of the Elizabethan age and is forever associated with one of the men whose life encapsulates that age: Sir Philip Sidney.

The Sidneys came to prominence under the Tudors. Sir William Sidney served Henry VIII as a soldier and a diplomat. His son Henry served both Edward VI and Mary as an able civil servant and wore himself out, physically and financially, in the service of Elizabeth. But it is for Henry's son Philip that the family is remembered.

Born in 1554 and named after his godfather Philip II of Spain (then the husband of Queen Mary), Philip was the quintessential renaissance man, brilliant, charming and heroic, who died young before court intrigue had chance to pull him down. Philip was a fine poet, whose major work, *Arcadia*, was inspired by the countryside around Penshurst. He was a witty and sparkling conversationalist and an excellent dancer, a sparkling courtier who soon became the favourite of Queen Elizabeth, and whose charm and smooth tongue enabled him to survive periodic falls from the monarch's grace. Philip died at the age of 32 from a wound received fighting the Spanish at the siege of Zutphen, an heroic if unnecessary end, which cemented his legend.

Philip lived much of his life at Penshurst, and even when he was a prominent courtier he would periodically retire to its tranquillity. It was here that he wrote most of his poetry and entertained friends, most famously his cousin Robert Dudley, Earl of Leicester, who unsuccessfully wooed Queen Elizabeth here.

## The Walk
This walk starts from the village of Leigh and passes through the Medway Valley that so inspired Philip Sidney's poetry, before reaching the Sidney home at Penshurst Place and returning across Penshurst Park.

- On the opposite side of the village green and cricket pitch from the main road is the club house of the local cricket team. Facing this clubhouse, take the road, signed as no through road, to the right of the clubhouse.
- Go up this short road, soon passing Lealands Avenue on your left.
- At the end of the road, go through a kissing gate and along a broad footpath, descending to cross under the railway.
- Continue along the footpath, now enclosed, for 60 yards, to a field gate. Go through the kissing gate beside the field gate and continue straight on along the field, keeping the fence to your right.
- Where the fence ends, proceed half-left across the field, towards a metal footbridge seen ahead.
- Cross the bridge over the River Medway and bear left for 50 yards with the path, to cross a footbridge on the right.

*The Medway traditionally divides Kentish Men from Men of Kent: the former are born to the west of the river, the latter to the east.*

- Ignore a left turn but go straight on for 30 yards to a squeeze stile into a field.
- Bear half right and follow the field edge for 20 yards to cross another stile.

- Keep straight on along the bottom of a very large field, keeping the hedge on the right, for nearly quarter of a mile, to eventually cross a stile onto a road.
- Turn right along the road and cross the Medway again. Immediately after crossing the bridge, turn left through a squeeze stile onto the river bank.
- Follow the river bank for quarter of a mile, keeping the river close on your left.
- Thirty yards after passing through a line of hawthorns, turn right at a waymark and cross the meadow to a footbridge visible in the hedge opposite.
- Cross the footbridge and bear half-left up the bank.
- Follow marker posts across the field to a stile, with a cluster of houses on your left.
- Cross the stile, turn right for 10 yards, then turn left at a T-junction onto a concrete drive.
- Follow the concrete drive for quarter of a mile through fields. When the drive turns sharp left, keep straight on down a grassy track.
- After 80 yards, pass through a squeeze stile into a field.
- Bear half-left across the field, crossing the brow of the hill (Penshurst Place now becomes visible ahead) and aiming for a stile in the bottom left corner of the field.
- Go through a squeeze stile, down the left-hand side of a field, and through a second stile onto a road.
- Turn right along the road. After a quarter of a mile, do not turn into the car park, but continue straight on, passing the walls of Penshurst Place on your right.
- Pass through the archway of the old gatehouse onto the road.
- Turn right along the road for 25 yards, then turn right up the steps and into the forecourt of Leicester Square.

*Penshurst village, just slightly further up the road, is a fine cluster of old houses and a inn, many dating from Tudor times. The best of the buildings are the half-timbered cottages that form a huge inhabited lychgate to the church and are known as Leicester Square, named after the Earl of Leicester. (Exactly which Earl it commemorates is debatable: it is probably Robert Sidney, who built the final major extensions to Penshurst Place, although some sources romantically believe it is Robert Dudley, cousin to the Sidneys and Queen Elizabeth's favourite, who spent much time here with the Queen.)*

*The ending 'hurst' is a common one for villages in Kent and means 'wooded hill', a reminder that the great Wealdan Forest covered most of the county at one time. Many settlements grew up in the forest, as men moved ever further into the trees in search of timber, charcoal and grazing. place names ending in 'ton', 'ing', 'ley' and 'ham' reflect this.*

- Pass though the archway ahead and into the churchyard, and bear left to the porch door.

*The Church of St John the Baptist is 13th century in origin, built out of sandstone with vast pinnacles on the Perpendicular tower. The nave has 13th and 14th-century arcades of the style known as Early English, with Victorian additions. Inside the church is the Chapel to the Sidney Family, built in 1820 and containing a history of the family. The tomb of Sir William Sidney is in the church, but the most famous of the Sidneys, Philip, is not here: he is buried in St Pauls Cathedral. There is a collection of 13th-century coffin lids.*

- Bear left around the church and follow a box hedge to a stile in the far corner of the churchyard.
- Cross the stile and bear half-right across the park, keeping a fence on your right. When the fence ends, keep the moat and wall on your right.
- Where the moat and wall swing away to the right, keep straight on to a gate seen in the fence ahead.

*Penshurst Place started life as a mediaeval manor house, built about 1340 by a London wool merchant Sir John de Pulteney, a mediaeval magnate who was four times Lord Mayor of London and who died in 1349 as a result of the Black Death. This stone house still forms the south front of the present building and contains Pulteney's Great Hall, 60 feet high with beams that are of chestnut rather than the usual oak and are supported by grotesque carvings of human figures. In 1430 it was bought by John Duke of Bedford, brother of Henry V, who*

**Penshurst Place, country retreat of soldier, poet and courtier Sir Phillip Sidney.**

*enlarged the building by adding the south-eastern wing known as the Buckingham Building. The house later passed to John's brother Humphrey, Duke of Gloucester.*

*In 1527 it was given by Edward VI to Sir William Sidney, a distinguished soldier and diplomat. He had fought at Flodden Field against the Scots and attended Henry VIII at the Field of the Cloth of Gold, the resplendent meeting in 1520 where the English and French kings sought a lasting peace. (Also present was Sir John Peche, owner of nearby Lullingstone Castle, see walk 6.) William's son Henry Sidney was a boyhood companion of the king's young son, Prince Edward. Henry Sidney really established Penshurst as the family seat, adding the north and west fronts and building the State Dining Room onto the older mediaeval hall. The house was enlarged into a magnificent renaissance palace by Henry Sidney's younger son Robert, who extended the house southwards with the Long and Nether galleries.*

*Both Robert and his son, also Robert, continued the family tradition of royal service for both James I and Charles I. But of the next generation, two sons fought against the king in the Civil War, while a third helped depose James II.*

*As well as its architectural interests, the house contains a collection of tapestries, furniture and paintings, and also an armoury with a collection of mediaeval and Elizabethan arms, including the helmet of Sir Philip Sidney There is also a toy museum.*

**Penshurst Place is privately owned and is open from April to September, 1–5.30pm daily, except Mondays. There is an admission charge.**

● Pass through a squeeze stile onto the drive. Cross the drive and exit through a second squeeze stile.

*Hunting was a passion of the aristocracy. Deer and wild boar had once freely roamed the abundant forests of England, and although under the Norman Laws of the Forest they were the sole property of the king his nobles were allowed to enter the forest to hunt. By the end of the 15th century increasing demand for living space and for wood had resulted in drastic deforestation. Consequently, in order to continue hunting great landowners needed to enclose large swathes of land and stock them with their own deer herds. Penshurst Park is one of a number of parks that still contain deer descended from those Elizabethan herds.*

● Keep straight on down an avenue of trees, passing the cricket pitch to your right.
● On reaching a brick pillbox on your left, leave the avenue and drop half-right down to a stile in the fence ahead.

*Much of this area of Kent is studded with pillboxes dating from World War Two. Fears of invasion were high in 1940 and 1941, and pillboxes were built to command any wide open spaces that could provide a landing ground for German parachutists. The park was criss-crossed with wooden spiked fences to obstruct gliders, and covered by strategically placed pillboxes which could act as fire points.*

● Cross the stile and turn right. Curve around the lake to a stile.

- Cross the stile and bear half-left through an avenue of trees to reach a fence on the far side of the field.
- Turn left and follow the fence uphill to a stile.
- Go through the stile and keep straight on uphill for quarter of a mile, through an avenue of trees.
- At the top of the slope, turn right and follow a broad grassy track along the ridge for 600 yards to a stile.
- Cross the stile and continue down the avenue of trees for a further 600 yards to reach the end of the wood.
- Where the wood ends, you need to continue straight on across the field, aiming for a gate in the top left corner (the right of way actually follows the left-hand fence around).
- Cross a stile beside a gate and continue straight on down a clear track, descending to a road.
- Turn left along the road. In 250 yards pass the entrance to Leigh station.
- Continue for a further 200 yards to a T-junction. Turn right to follow the road back to the village green.

*It is worth staying to the right-hand side of the main road and observing the old dovecote preserved in the garden of a cottage just before you reach the post office, and also the old almshouses just beyond the post office.*

WALK 17

# Peckham: the first industrial revolution in the 16th century

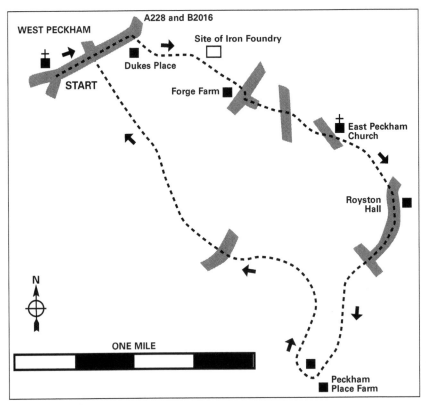

**Distance:** 4 miles

**Map:** OS sheet 188

**Start and Parking:** The walk starts from West Peckham Church (grid ref: 645526). West Peckham is five miles north-east of Tonbridge, on a minor road signposted just off the junction of the A26 and the B2016. There is limited parking in West Peckham near the church.

**Refreshments:** Public house in West Peckham.

## Historical Background

Travelling around Kent today it is hard to realise that in Tudor times the county was the industrial heart of England. This process had started in the 14th century, when Edward III settled Flemish weavers in Kent to start a cloth industry. The small towns and villages in the centre of Kent soon grew in prosperity, both through manufacturing cloth and raising sheep.

But the real take-off of Kentish industry came in the 16th century. Iron had been mined in the Weald since Roman times, but smelting had used foot-pumps and the resulting metal had been of poor quality. During the Tudor period the use of water-powered smelting was perfected, and the production of iron of a much higher quality began. The demand for Kentish iron exploded, driven at least in part by the need to service the new Royal Navy dockyards that Henry VIII founded around the Kentish coast in 1515. Ore was extracted, often using open-cast mining or shallow mines, and smelting plants sprang up on streams all over the Weald. Trees were cut down at an alarming rate to feed the charcoal-fired engines. As the supply of trees in an area was exhausted, the iron mills simply moved further into the forest, thereby accelerating the process of deforestation.

This can truly be called England's first Industrial Revolution, and Kent remained the industrial heart of England until the mid-18th century, when the invention of coal-powered machinery moved the focus to the coalfields of the Midlands and North.

The main centres of Tudor industrialisation were in the Weald, but the woods and streams of the Greensand Ridge also attracted their share of industry. The transient nature of the industry and subsequent redevelopment of the land have left little trace now on the ground. A few remains of the foundries can still be discovered, and memorials in some churches and the names of some of the farms and houses still bear witness to this forgotten chapter of the county's past.

## The Walk

**This walk starts in the interesting old village of West Peckham, passes the 'ghost-town' around East Peckham, and sees hints and traces of the first Industrial Revolution, while going through quiet and little-walked countryside.**

*West Peckham has an extensive village green, somewhat unusual in that it is not enclosed by buildings but remains open on one-and-a-half sides. St Dunstan's Church is Saxon in origin, with a Saxon tower containing a double-splayed Saxon window. The rest of the church dates mainly from Norman times. Inside the church there is a Squires Pew, built above the chancel, with its own separate entrance from the churchyard. It is panelled and comfortably furnished, and so high sided that it gives total privacy from the vicar as well as from the congregation.*

- With the church on your left, walk down the road, passing the village hall on your right.
- At a road junction, keep straight on down Mereworth Road.

St Dunstan's Church, West Peckham, dates from Saxon times.

● Follow the road, with houses on the right and a field on the left. The last house, shielded by high hedges, is Dukes Place.

*Dukes Place was believed to be a presbytery of the Knights Templar, who were granted land in West Peckham in the 1330s. The Templars were founded in AD1118 to protect travellers journeying through the Holy Land. Their name comes from the fact that their original headquarters was on top of the Temple Mound in Jerusalem.*

*The order grew in numbers and wealth, and when the loss of the Holy Land forced them to relocate to the West, they established themselves as bankers to the various monarchs. They grew in independence, wealth and arrogance and they eventually became hated by both clergy and secular authorities. The order were expelled from much of Europe in 1307 by the combined might of the Pope and King Philip IV of France, and moved their centre of operations into England and Germany instead. They never regained their former influence and power and gradually withered away as the Holy Land ceased to be an issue for European monarchs.*

● Immediately after Dukes Place, turn right down a concrete drive, at a footpath sign and waymark post.

● Where the concrete drive bends sharp right, keep straight on for 20 yards down a track and cross a stile on the left into a field.

● Cross the field half-left, aiming for a gate in the middle of the hedge on the opposite side.

● Do not go through the gate but turn right and follow the field boundary, keeping alongside the hedge on the left.

- Fifty yards before reaching the corner of the field, cross a stile on the left, and then continue along the same line down the edge of the field, now in an enclosed track.
- Cross over a footbridge and climb to a stile beyond.

*To the left just past the footbridge is an earthen bank, once the retaining wall of a small dam. Iron was mined at many locations throughout the county and worked in forges that relied on local waterpower and burnt charcoal that was available in abundance in the Wealdan Forest. This dam would have driven a water wheel which in turn would have powered either a forge hammer or the bellows for a charcoal furnace.*

*Iron was in increasing demand in the 16th and 17th centuries, to meet the ever-increasing needs of England's fleet. It was the cutting of oaks for warships and the burning of lesser trees for charcoal that led to the virtual deforestation of south-east England by the end of the 18th century.*

- Keep ahead towards a gate in the far-right corner of the field, beside a farm.
- Cross two stiles, the second next to the gate, and keep ahead up the track to pass to the left of the oast houses of Forge Farm and out to the main road.

*The name Forge Farm is another echo of the area's industrial past.*

- Turn right along the road for 50 yards and then turn left into a narrow lane, concreted initially but after 20 yards overgrown and grassy.
- Follow the lane for 300 yards and then cross a stile onto a road. Cross the road to the lane opposite and climb with the lane, winding uphill for 500 yards to reach a road junction with Old Church Lane.
- Cross the lane and go up a flight of steps to enter the churchyard by a stile, and pass around the church keeping it to your left.

*The village of Peckham was originally around what is now the Church of East Peckham. The area was abandoned when the settlement moved two miles west to what is now West Peckham, in order to be near the river which was the source of waterpower and hence employment in the 16th century. The church was abandoned but restored in the 19th century.*

- Ignore a path leading down to the lychgate but keep around the side of the church for a further 10 yards, and then turn right down a narrow path through the gravestones to a narrow gateway in the churchyard wall.
- Go through the gate and bear left, keeping the wall on your left, to cross a stile into a field.
- Go half-left down the field the opposite side. Turn right, keeping the field boundary on your left, to reach a stile.
- Cross two stiles in quick succession. Follow an enclosed path downhill, skirting a conifer plantation, and reach a stile in front of Royston Hall.

*Royston Hall was built in 1535 but little of the original building remains. The west front that can be seen through the gate is original in parts, although even here later alterations have blurred its lines.*

- Turn right down the road, passing the rear entrance to the hall, and follow the lane until you reach a T-junction.
- Cross the road and go through a gate opposite at a footpath sign. Go straight on across the field to a stile in the opposite fence.
- Cross the stile and go ahead for 15 yards through scrub to reach a field edge.
- Turn left and walk with a conifer hedge on your left.
- When the hedge ends, maintain the same line of advance across the field, passing an isolated tree on your left, and then soon picking up a line of trees on your left.
- Descend the field to the corner. Ignore a gap on the left but keep ahead through a gap in the hedge in front to reach a fence and a stile crossing into the field on your right.
- Cross the stile and go half-left across the field to a gap in the hedge in the bottom corner, aiming at the buildings seen in the trees beyond.
- Go through the hedge and cross a narrow stone footbridge.
- Follow a clear grassy track to the corner of a drive.
- Keep straight on up the drive, passing outbuildings on your right and leaving the farm and ponds away on your left.
- Go through the gates (labelled Peckham Place Farm) and immediately turn right onto a track.
- After 100 yards, at a junction of tracks where the fence on the right ends, turn right onto a track.
- Follow the track through a band of trees and across a large field.
- Eighty yards short of the far side of the field, turn left at a waymark post (Weald Way) and follow the footpath across the field.
- Cross a stile and go half-left across the next field. At the far side cross over a farm track and climb a stile onto the road.
- Cross the road half-right to a stile at a footpath sign.
- Cross a brick bridge to a stile beyond. Go over a cross track with a gate on the left and keep ahead, to enter a fenced track.
- Follow the track, with a ditch on the left, and keep straight on, soon to enter a field.
- Keep straight on along the edge of the field, with a ditch on the left.
- On the far side of the field cross a stile and then bear half-right across the field, aiming for a stile in a clump of trees seen on the far side.
- Maintain the same line of advance across the next field, aiming for a stile in the top right corner of the field.
- Maintain the same line of advance across the next field, then cross a stile and continue up the left-hand edge of another field, to enter an enclosed footpath.
- Follow the footpath to a gate at a road junction. Turn left and follow the lane back to West Peckham Church.

WALK 18

# Chilham: the evolution of a village from pre-historic times to the 17th century

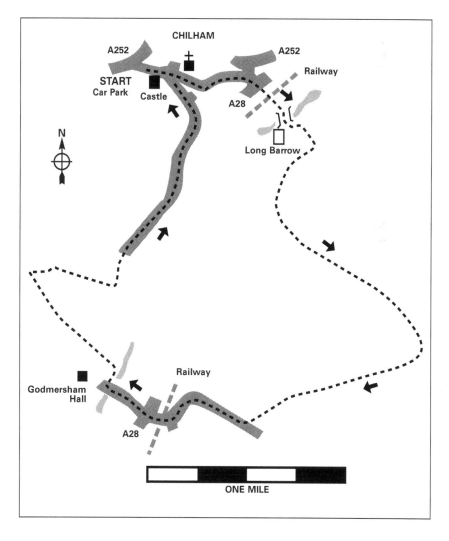

**Distance:** 5 miles
**Map:** OS sheet 189
**Start and Parking:** The walk starts from the free car park on the north side of Chilham village (grid ref: 066537). Chilham is just off the A252, seven miles south of Canterbury. Drive west along the A252 and take the second turn to Chilham, and the car park is immediately off the main road.
**Refreshments:** Public houses and tearooms and a shop in Chilham.

### Historical Background

Chilham was built in a commanding position on a hilltop, easily defensible, and near one of the main routes connecting Canterbury to London. The hill had been used by the Romans as an army camp during Julius Caesar's second invasion in 54BC, offering as it did a defensible site on high ground above the marshy River Stour valley, on the line of Caesar's advance from the channel coast towards the Thames valley. After the Conquest, the Romans settled in the area.

Chilham later became a Saxon stronghold, possibly of a local lord named Cille (in Saxon Chilham means the 'ham' or settlement of Cille). Although most of the area was covered by the great Wealdan Forest, itself a source of wealth for those communities able to exploit it, Chilham stood on the banks the River Stour with its rich and fertile agricultural land.

Chilham was a settled community from at least Saxon times, and its layout is a splendid example of Saxon society recorded in buildings. The houses of the village clustered around a central square on the top of the hill with roads leading off from each corner. On one side of the square was the castle, originally a wood and earth fortification of the local Saxon lord, but later a more substantial stone-built structure for the village's Norman landlords. On the other side of the square stood the church. The twin powers of church and lord dominate the village and the landscape.

The prosperity of Chilham grew over time, and its wood and earth Saxon dwellings were replaced by more substantial stone and later brick buildings. The market square and the four lanes leading off it, one in each corner, are today lined with buildings from the Tudor and Jacobean era and is little altered since that time.

### The Walk

This walk starts in the perfectly-preserved village of Chilham and then crosses the River Stour to ramble through the hills opposite, with fine views over Chilham. It returns via Godmersham Park, with its associations with Jane Austin.

● From the car park turn right into the lane and walk up to the village street. Continue to the main village square, with tearooms on the left and the castle gates on the right.

*The site of Chilham Castle was originally a Roman and then a Saxon stronghold, a fortified earthworks with wooden palisades. After the Norman Conquest, the land was granted by William the Conqueror to his half brother Odo, Bishop of Bayeaux, who also held estates at*

The market square at Chilham is surrounded by fine Tudor and Jacobean buildings.

*Chevening (see walk 19) and at Rochester (see walk 8). Odo started by building a simple motte and bailey castle here, an earthen mound with a wooden palisade around it. In the 12th century the land passed to a Norman knight, Fulbert de Lacy, whose daughter married a bastard son of King John. De Lacy extended the castle, building one of the only two octagonal keeps in England. The castle became Crown property during the Wars of the Roses, when the then owner Lord Rees was convicted of treason.*

*The castle fell into disrepair, and in 1616 the Norman ruins were largely pulled down and replaced with a new castle by the then owner Sir Dudley Digges, Master of Roles to James I. Built to designs by Inigo Jones, and constructed largely of brick on the unusual ground plan of five sides of a hexagon, this is one of the finest examples of a Jacobean castle and gardens in England. The garden designs were modified by the famous landscape gardener Capability Brown and contained the first wisteria in Britain.*

The gardens used to be open to the public. At the time of writing this is no longer so, although this may change in the future.

- With your back to the castle gates, walk down the square to the entrance to the church, beside the White Horse public house.

*Although St Mary's Church originated in Saxon times, the present building dates from the 14th century and it was much rebuilt in the Victorian era. It has a flint Perpendicular tower.*

*Chilham was on the Pilgrims' route and the church was used by worshippers en route to Canterbury. In 1538, when St Augustine's Abbey in Canterbury was dissolved, the gilded shrine containing St Augustine's bones was brought to Chilham but disappeared a few years later. Today the church houses many monuments to the former residents of Chilham Castle, the Digges Family, and some fine stained-glass windows.*

● Facing the entrance to the churchyard and the White Horse, turn right and walk down The Street, with the church off to your left and passing between Clements Cottage and Chantry House. Descend The Street.

*It is worth strolling slowly down The Street and taking the time to look at the fine Tudor and Jacobean buildings you pass. The other streets leading off the square are worth exploration either now or on your return to Chilham at the end of the walk.*

● Pass The Woolpack on your right and bear left with The Street. Ignore all side roads and follow The Street out of the village, to reach the A252 in a quarter of a mile.
● Pass a spur onto the A252 on your left and follow The Street as it bears around to the right and in 100 yards reaches a T-junction with the A28, opposite a garage.
● Cross the A28 and continue straight on down a no through road, passing the garage on your right. In 50 yards cross the railway.
● Follow the road across a bridge over the River Stour and bear right up a fenced drive, passing Mill House on the left.
● Cross a second bridge and turn left into a track.
● At the gates to a cottage, turn left and follow a footpath along the river bank, soon climbing through trees to reach a cross track.

*In the field behind the cottage is a Neolithic long barrow or burial mound. The mound was reopened in the third century AD and the bodies of a Roman adult and two children were buried in it, possibly affluent Romano-British settlers who lived in the vicinity. The site is now called Julliberrie Down, named after Julius Laverius, a Roman officer who was part of Caesar's second expeditionary force and who died in a skirmish with British guerrillas near the same spot in 54BC. Despite a local legend, neither Laverius nor any other Roman soldiers are buried in the mound.*

● Cross over the cross track and continue ahead up a grassy track, which soon narrows to become a path and leads into a field.
● Keep forward along the left-hand edge of the field. Follow the field edge around two sides to cross a stile on the edge of the wood.
● Turn right along a track, which is initially tree-lined, then with a field to the right, then tree-lined again. Reach a cross track, with a concrete footpath sign on the left.
● Turn left and climb up the cross track for 15 yards to a field gate.
● Go through the field gate and follow a broad path half-right across the field towards woods.
● On reaching the woods, turn left with the track and proceed with trees on your right. After 25 yards, turn right into trees, still on the broad track.
● Pass through a band of woodland to emerge into a field. Turn left and follow the left-hand edge of the field uphill.

- At the top of the field keep straight on through a band of trees into another field.
- Turn right and follow the right-hand edge of the field, walking along the bottom of the field with a hedge on your right, for 100 yards, to reach a waymark post on the right.
- With your back to the post, walk half-right across the field, contouring around the slope and avoiding climbing towards the trees on your left. Soon you reach a stile in the hedge ahead.
- Cross the stile and descend along a clear path through scrubland. The path is soon enclosed by hedges and in 50 yards reaches a stile.
- Cross the stile and keep straight on along the hedged footpath between fields.
- At a cross track, where the path starts climbing deeper into the trees, turn right onto a narrower waymarked footpath through trees, with a field over the fence on the right.
- Cross a stile and keep straight on along the bottom of a field, with the field boundary on the right. At the end of the field, cross over a track to a stile.
- Cross the stile and keep ahead along a narrow footpath through trees.
- In 150 yards, turn right at a waymarked post and gently descend with the path into a field.
- Keep straight on down the right-hand edge of the field. At the bottom of slope, cross a ladder stile and immediately turn right to cross two metal gates in quick succession. After the second gate go half-left across the field to a stile in the left-hand fence.
- Cross the stile to go up an enclosed footpath for 50 yards to reach a track.
- Turn right and follow the track, soon passing between buildings. When the track becomes metalled, and just after exiting through gates, turn left over a stile into a field.
- Go half-right up the field, aiming for a stile visible on the horizon in the top-right corner of the field.
- Cross the stile, with a buried reservoir to the right, and go straight ahead into a field.
- Follow the right edge of the field for 130 yards, then turn right through the hedge and then immediately turn left, to continue the former line of advance, now with the hedge on your left.

*There are fine views of Chilham over to your right, clearly demonstrating its commanding hilltop position. In mediaeval times, when most of the land would have been forested, occasional glimpses of Chilham would have been visible through the trees, in particular views of those two symbols of feudal authority which still dominate the view of the village, namely the church and the castle.*

- At a waymark post in 120 yards, turn half-right and descend across a large field, following a vague path, to descend steeply through a gap in the hedge.
- Continue the same line of advance across the next large field to reach a stile in the bottom corner onto a lane.
- Turn right along the lane for half a mile. At a T-junction of lanes, turn right under a railway bridge and go up the lane for 300 yards to reach the main road.

- Cross the main road and continue down the road opposite, signposted to Godmersham Church.
- Cross a bridge and go ahead to the right-hand set of gates beside the lodge opposite. Pass through a pedestrian gate and immediately turn right through a wooden gate.
- Keep ahead across the park for 170 yards, initially with a fence on the left, then continue straight ahead where the fence ends, aiming for another fence ahead. Follow this fence for a few yards, then turn left through a gate and up an enclosed drive.

*To the left is the house of Godmersham Park, built in 1732 by Thomas Brodnax and later home of his cousin Edward Knight, Jane Austin's brother (who had to change his name to Knight in order to inherit Godmersham). Jane was a frequent visitor to Godmersham but, as her letters reveal, she considered the people she met during her visits neither her cultural nor her intellectual equals. She used the house and the society she encountered there as models for many scenes in* Mansfield Park *and* Pride and Prejudice.

- After 200 yards, at a junction of tracks, keep straight on, passing the entrance to Deer Lodge on your right.
- Climb with the track, cross a stile and bear right.
- After 30 yards, stop following the track but bear half-right across the hill, aiming first for a marker post in the field and then to a stile beyond.
- Cross the stile and maintain the same line of advance across the field beyond, aiming for a marker post at the edge of the woods ahead.
- Cross the stile into the woods. Immediately turn right and follow a track along the edge of the woods.
- Go through a kissing gate beside a field gate and turn right along a cross track, still following the edge of the woods, now downhill.
- Leave the wood and follow an enclosed track downhill.
- Follow the track, now tree-lined, as it bends left around a corner. Follow the track, ignoring all turns to the left, to reach a lane.
- Keep ahead down the lane. Follow it for three quarters of a mile, until you reach School Lane on the left.
- Go up School Lane into Chilham Square. Pass the castle gates on the left and turn left down the hill back to the car park.

WALK 19
# Chevening: landscapes and landowners in Georgian times

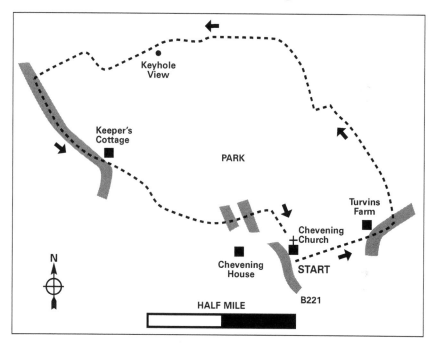

**Distance:** 4.5 miles

**Map:** OS sheet 188

**Start and parking:** The walk starts from St Botolph's Church, Chevening (grid ref: 489577). To reach Chevening, leave the A25 at Sunbridge and go north along the B221 signed Chevening. After two miles turn left (north) off the B road up a minor road signed Chevening. There is limited parking in the village outside the church.

**Refreshments:** None

### Historical Background

Very often the physical landscape as we now see it has been moulded by the wishes of great landowners of the past. In our towns and cities the evidence of this is often now obscured by modern development of the land, but in rural areas clear examples are still to be found.

While Chevening Park has never been one of the great estates of England, it contains some good illustrations of how generations of landowners have left their mark on the countryside.

The village of Chevening itself was built by the then lord of the manor to house his retainers, and to this day it remains the property of the Chevening Estate. The Church of St Botolph's, at the end of the carriageway from Chevening House, was greatly extended by later landowners to provide a chapel for their tombs. Ancient roadways were diverted to remove them from the lord's grounds. The park was extensively re-landscaped to meet the recreational requirements of the owners.

Chevening House itself, built between 1616 and 1630, is a good example of a country seat, conveniently close to London and used by generations of administrators as somewhere to relax after toiling in the capital.

**The Walk**
**This walk passes Chevening House, a superb example of the classical design, and climbs along the North Downs escarpment for some exhilarating views over the park and surrounding countryside, before descending through woods and back into Chevening Park.**

- Enter St Botoph's churchyard via the lychgate. Pass through the churchyard with the church on your left. Where the path divides, keep straight on to exit the churchyard via a gate.

*There has been a church on this site since at least 1122, when the parish was still known by its Saxon name of Civilinga. The oldest part of the present St Botoph's Church dates from the 13th century, when the nave and chancel were enlarged. The tower and typically Kentish turret were built in 1518. A chapel was added in 1585 by John Lennard of Chevening Place and ever since has housed the monumental tombs of the Lennard and Stanhope families.*

- Keep straight on along an enclosed track to cross a stile into a field.
- Continue along the left-hand edge of the field to enter a second enclosed track. Keep straight on to reach a road.
- Turn left along the road to pass Turvins farm.
- Follow the road, 100 yards past Turvins farm, turn left over a stile and walk along an enclosed path.
- Leave the enclosed path over a stile. Continue straight on up the right-hand edge of the field. At the top of the field, turn left with the hedge for 20 yards, then turn right up some steps to a stile.
- Cross the stile and follow the hedge up the right side of the field. At the top of the field, turn left and continue straight on along the top of three fields, keeping the woods to your right and views to your left. There are 'North Downs Way' signs at intervals along your route.

St Botolph's Church at Chevening.

- Near the end of the third field, turn uphill, following the right-hand edge of the field, still with woods on your right, to reach a stile on the right, beside a gate.
- Cross the stile and walk forward and quarter left, aiming for the corner of a wood 100 yards ahead.
- Turn left around the corner of the wood and follow the field edge, keeping the woods on your left, for a quarter of a mile.
- Where the field boundary swings slightly right, ignore a kissing gate in the corner but swing right with the hedge for 10 yards, to cross a stile on the left.
- Follow the path for 200 yards through a wood. At the end bear left with the path and enter a field
- Turn right along the right-hand edge of the field. Cross it, keeping the hedge to your right, to a gate.
- Pass through the gate, turn right for 10 yards, then turn left into a large field.
- Keep straight on, following the left-hand edge of the large field to enter a second field.
- Proceed for 100 yards along the left-hand edge of the field, to the famous 'keyhole view' of Chevening on your left.

*In 1769 Lord Chatham borrowed Chevening as a residence from its owner, his cousin, the 2nd Earl Stanhope, and built a carriageway through the park, to provide easy recreational riding. As part of this scheme, he had a 'keyhole' cut through the woods above Chevening to provide a view down over the house when resting from his exertions.*

- Continue along the left-hand edge of the large field, going around nearly two sides of it, to reach a stile on the left into woodland.
- Cross the stile and follow the path for quarter of a mile through the edge of the woodland, to reach a field.
- Turn left and follow the edge of the field for 200 yards to reach a road.
- Turn left into the road, and walk down it for half a mile, until Keepers Cottage is reached on your left.
- Pass the cottage, and immediately turn left through the yard and proceed straight ahead along a broad and intermittently-metalled track into the woods.
- Follow the track for quarter of a mile. When the track reaches a gate and the metalling ends, turn right with the track, now grassy.
- Follow this grassy track for 150 yards to reach a field.
- Continue down the left-hand edge of the field to cross a stile, and then continue through a narrow strip of woodland.

*There is an excellent view from this point down across Chevening Park to Chevening Place and beyond it, to St Botolph's Church. The original route of the Pilgrims' Way crossed the park directly in front of the house but was diverted by the 3rd Earl Stanhope to the top of the North Downs ridge. Another ancient right of way, the Fish Route, used for transporting fish from Rye to London, ran parallel to the drive that now leads to the house. This too was diverted out of the park, to the east.*

- Enter the field and descend the left-hand edge of the field to reach a kissing gate.
- Pass through the gate and turn left onto a track.
- Follow the track downhill with woods on the left and Chevening House on the right. Immediately before reaching a farm track ahead, turn right over a stile.
- Continue down the left-hand edge of the field, keeping the farm track to your left to reach the main drive to Chevening House. Cross the drive using stiles.

*You are now crossing the carriageway laid down by Lord Chatham, which is still known as Chatham Drive. The original course of the Pilgrims' Way was along the foot of the slope you have just descended.*

*Chevening Place was the country estate of Bishop Odo of Bayeaux, half-brother of William the Conqueror, who accompanied the invading Normans in 1066 as father confessor to the army. Odo, who commissioned the Bayeaux Tapestry to commemorate the successful Norman invasion of Britain, acted as Regent of Britain whenever William had to return to Normandy, and also had considerable ecclesiastical duties in the newly-conquered territories. Odo lived and ruled from his palace in Greenwich, conveniently close to the capital, but used his estates in Chevening as a place to relax from the affairs of state. Odo also built the castle at Chilham (see walk 18) and the first castle at Rochester (see walk 8).*

*From Odo the estate passed to Adam de Chevening, a Norman baron who built the original village on his land for his retainers. It then passed through the hands of four families before being bought by the Lennards in 1551. It was the 13th Baron Lennard who commissioned the famous Stuart architect Inigo Jones to rebuild the house in its present form.*

*In 1715 the house passed to the Stanhope family, who were industrious public servants for much of the later Stuart and early Hanoverian period. General James Stanhope was a soldier, diplomat and parliamentarian and was rewarded with the title Earl Stanhope. Charles, 3rd Earl Stanhope, was a notable patron of science and technology and a brilliant scientist himself. He invented a calculating machine which was to be the forerunner of Babbage's famous calculator, from which modern computers are descended. Charles also closed down the two ancient trackways, the Fish Route and the Pilgrims' Way, and diverted them outside the boundaries of the estate, where they would be less inconvenient to him.*

*In 1959 Chevening House was bequested to the nation by the 7th Earl Stanhope, to be used as a residence either for Cabinet ministers or for descendants of King George I. Between 1974 and 1980 Prince Charles lived in Chevening.*

- Keep straight on, keeping the fence to your right, until a wood is reached ahead. Turn left along the front of the wood and follow the edge of the wood to a stile on to a private drive.
- Cross the drive by stiles to enter a field. Keep straight on along the right-hand edge of the field to reach a stile.
- Cross the stile and turn right into an enclosed footpath. Follow the footpath between fields and through a horse barrier until it emerges on to a drive opposite the gate into St Botolph's churchyard.
- Enter the churchyard and follow the path, keeping the church on your right, back to the lychgate.

WALK 20

# Upnor: coastal defences during the 17th century

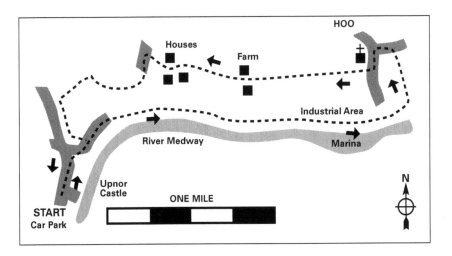

**Distance:** 5.5 miles

**Map:** OS sheet 178

**Start and Parking:** The walk starts from the car park in Upnor Village (grid ref: 757706). Upnor is two miles north-east of Strood, on a minor road clearly signposted off the A228 Strood–Grain road. Follow signs for the village and Castle, and the car park is on your right as you approach the town.

**Refreshments:** Public houses in Upnor.

### Historical Background

The River Medway has been associated with the Royal Navy ever since the latter was created by Henry VIII in 1515. Initially the river was used to provide secure and sheltered anchorage for vessels that were 'laid up', that is, not in active service. Provisioning facilities were available, and very soon ship-building and boat-repair yards were developed. By the start of Elizabeth I's reign, Chatham was the foremost Royal Naval yard in England. Vessels that were laid up were without masts and rigging, and so were highly vulnerable, and in 1559 Queen Elizabeth ordered the building of a fort at Upnor to protect Chatham and the Medway anchorage from attack. The original castle was completed by 1564, and reinforced in 1585, when open war with Spain was declared.

The castle never saw active service during Elizabeth's reign but remained central to the defences of the Medway throughout the Stuart era. It saw its only action in 1667, during the Second Dutch War. Lulled into a false sense of security after defeating the Dutch at sea, the English fleet were laid up in Chatham as an economy measure. Against expectations, the Dutch, under Admiral de Ruyter, sailed up the Medway, burned the unfinished fort at Sheerness and threatened Chatham itself. Upnor Castle put up a spirited defence but was unable to prevent part of the English fleet being burned and the flagship, the *Royal Sovereign*, being carried off by the Dutch.

The Medway defences were drastically overhauled after this disaster. New forts and gun platforms were built further downstream, and Upnor became redundant. In 1668 the fort was converted into a gunpowder magazine. It was used both as this and as a barracks until 1827, servicing the English fleet throughout the wars of the 18th century and the Napoleonic wars.

### The Walk

**Although this walk is probably the least scenic in this series, it does contain much of historical interest. It starts at Upnor castle and goes along the Medway, passing various stages of the river's defences and going through the marinas and boatyards for which the banks of the Medway are used today. It returns through pleasant agricultural land and across the high ground above Upnor.**

- Leave the car park by the pedestrian exit, signposted 'Castle and Village', at the opposite end of the car park to the car access. Go out onto the road.
- Before starting the walk proper, make a small detour to Upnor castle. Go straight ahead down the old High Street, past old weatherboarded houses and pubs.

*The village of Upnor is little more than one street. It is actually only 400 years old as a settlement, which grew up outside the walls of the Tudor castle to provide taverns for the garrison and married quarters for the troops.*

- At the end of the High Street is a bench with a fine view over Chatham Dockyard and the Medway Anchorage. The entrance to Upnor Castle is immediately on your left.

*The buildings you can see around the present gateway into the castle are a brick-built three-storey barracks. They were built in 1718 to replace the former accommodation in the castle, when this was taken over to provide storage for gunpowder. Parliament had been wary about constructing permanent bases for a standing army ever since military power had been abused by the Stuarts, and these were among the first purpose-built barracks to be constructed in England. Beside the barracks is the 18th-century guardroom.*

*The castle itself is hidden from sight. It has evolved over time and was originally, in Tudor times, a small rectangular building designed to provide a simple gun platform. Looking out across the river to the site of the Tudor dockyards on the opposite bank, you can appreciate how these guns would have commanded the entrance into the anchorage. The defences were increased by building a strong gatehouse and curtain wall on the landward side, with a dry ditch around the outside. When the castle was converted into a gunpowder magazine in 1667, the frontage onto the river was drastically modified, the courtyard redesigned and the interior extensively altered.*

**Upnor Castle is open from April to October, 10am–4pm. There is an admission fee but it is free to members of English Heritage.**

- To start the walk proper, retrace your steps up the High Street to the car park pedestrian entrance. Do not enter the car park but turn right, away from the Kings Arms, and follow the road.
- At a road junction in 80 yards, keep straight on, immediately passing the gates to Upper Castle House, and bear off right on a footpath, with the walls of the house on your right.

*The house to the right was the official residence of the storekeeper of the Upnor Magazine. Once the castle ceased to be the front line of defence, there was no need for a full strength garrison or for a commanding officer to live in the fort itself. The garrison was now from the ordnance corps, and the commander was officially a 'storekeeper', for whom a separate and quite luxurious residence was built.*

- Eventually descend some steps with the footpath onto a road. Turn right and follow the road around past the gates to the dockyard and past a boatyard.
- Pass The Ship public house, and immediately opposite at The Pier public house bear right away from the road onto a footpath that stays to the riverside.
- Pass an obelisk on the left and pass between metal posts onto a drive. Keep straight on along the drive, and go through the first set of gates marked 'Medway Yacht Club', but at the next set of gates bear right and follow the footpath between the river and a fence.
- At the end of the fence the path descends to the shoreline for a few yards and then climbs steeply up the bank into the trees.
- At the top of the bank, keep the same direction across an open area for 10 yards, and then go through a gap in the fence onto a footpath through the woods.
- Follow a clear track that winds through the trees, keeping the shoreline between five yards and 30 yards away to your right. Follow the woodland path for a mile.
- The path leaves the trees, where there is a sign announcing 'gas mains under river' on your left, and a white jetty marks the boundary of permanent moorings.

*Where you are now standing was the site of the Cockham Wood Fort, and the low flat island seen behind the marina is Hoo Ness. Even prior to 1667 there had been a chain stretched between Hoo Ness and the opposite (eastern) bank of the Medway. This was immensely thick, capable of being lowered and raised, and designed to block one of the two channels up the Medway and force all ships to enter by the western channel, under the guns of Upnor.*

The gatehouse to Upnor Castle, built in 1718 to replace the original Tudor building.

*After the humiliation of 1667, new defences were built to strengthen the Medway. Two new gun batteries were built, one here at Cockham Wood and one on the opposite bank, at Gillingham. In addition, a smaller battery was built on Hoo Ness itself. Between them, these three batteries could command the entrance to the upper Medway, and enemy vessels would have been under constant fire as they manoeuvred slowly through the shoals and mud flats of the river.*

- Continue ahead along the footpath, with grass lawns edged with telegraph poles on your left and permanent houseboat moorings on your right.
- Pass through gates and continue along the drive towards the marina. Where the drive swings left through some gates, continue straight on along the footpath at a concrete footpath marker. The footpath soon becomes enclosed with a hedge on the left and a fence on the right.
- Do not enter the marina but keep ahead with the fence intermittently on your right and prefabs on your left.
- Ignore a drive to your left but keep ahead, passing to the right of a yellow-brick and corrugated-iron building.
- Pass garages on your right and keep ahead up the track, with the link fence of a boatyard on your immediate right. Bear left with the fence to cross the entrance of Hoo Marina. Ignore a drive to the left and keep ahead, still parallel with the river, to pass through small industrial units.
- The path soon becomes enclosed again, with a concrete fence on the left, and then emerges into a tarmacked parking and turning area. Ahead is a fence surrounding a boatyard, while to your right an open field is visible 50 yards away.
- Turn left and walk up a tarmacked drive for 50 yards. Where the drive turns left, keep ahead following the signposted footpath across a field.

*Pause on this path and look over your right shoulder, towards the power station downstream. In the estuary beyond was Fort Darnet, a gun battery built in 1668 on a mud flat in midstream. Another battery stood on the mudflats beyond the power station, and these two, in combination with the batteries at Cockham Wood and Hoo Ness, would have laid down a deadly fire upon any enemy ship trying to force its way up river. In addition, huge sharpened poles were sunk into the mud at low water, designed to rip the bottom out of any vessel trying to go close to the shore to avoid the barrage from the batteries.*

- Opposite the church, you should ignore a footpath to the left (it is not a right of way) but keep straight on until the houses ahead are reached.
- Turn left in front of the houses and follow the road for 100 yards to a T-junction.
- Turn left in the main road for 60 yards, and then turn right onto a footpath into the churchyard.
- Follow the footpath through the churchyard, keeping the church on your left, to exit at the end of the churchyard. Do not turn left into a new housing estate, but turn right down an enclosed footpath for 30 yards to reach an open field.

- Turn left in the field and follow the boundary for 20 yards to reach a metalled track.
- Turn right along the track. After half a mile pass through a gate and keep straight on past a barn on the right, to come to a junction of tracks in front of a farmhouse. Do not turn down towards the farmhouse but keep ahead, passing a large chicken house on your left, walking with a line of trees on your right.
- A quarter of a mile past the farm, ignore a footpath going off to your right but keep ahead along the track. The track soon passes between trees on the right and the wall of a house on the left.
- At the house gates do not turn right down the drive but keep straight on along a footpath beside a wall. Follow the footpath, soon enclosed, out to a road.
- Turn left along the road. In 100 yards, at a turning point at the road end, keep straight on down a track, which soon becomes a footpath. Follow the footpath downhill and curve right.
- Just around the bend, do not go down shallow steps on your right, but follow the path as it curves rightwards and descends, soon passing a seat with a magnificent view over the Medway.

*On the opposite bank of the river you can see the old Royal Naval Dockyard at Chatham, currently being restored to its 18th-century state, and open to the public. The red-brick building on the waterfront that you can see was the gatehouse to the Royal Naval Yard, built in 1726 by Sir John Vanbrugh. Behind the gatehouse you can see the sheds which housed the sailmaking shops, while the long, low building housed the ropemaking shop. The harbour front would have been alive with derricks for replacing masts and replenishing supplies, while behind were dry docks for more drastic repairs.*

*Upnor Castle can be seen on the waterfront down to your right, and its strategic position, commanding the entrance to the dockyards in Tudor times, can be appreciated. After 1668 it became a gunpowder magazine. The powder was stored on the opposite side of the river to the warships and dockyards, in case of an accidental explosion. Small boats or 'lighters' would have been rowed across the river from the warships at anchor off Chatham and collected supplies of gunpowder.*

*To your left and just around the bend in the river were the batteries of Cockham Wood and Hoo Ness, the Medway's defences after 1668. In addition, two further batteries were located in the woods, along the ridge you are now standing on, to provide yet another field of fire to be poured into any attacker. The Admiralty was determined that any repetition of the humiliation of 1667 would be avoided at all costs!*

- Follow the path as it gently descends. At a T-junction, with a path on the left and steps and a path on the right, turn right and climb, keeping to the left-hand boundary of an open grassy area.
- In 60 yards cross a stile ahead and climb through trees. Follow the path through trees until it crosses a footbridge, and five yards later a stile.
- Cross the stile and turn right along an enclosed footpath. In 200 yards cross the top of a drive and continue straight on through a gate.

The cannon at Upnor commanded the entrance to Chatham and the Medway.

- Descend the path, still enclosed, with an iron fence on the left and the boundary of archery club land on your right. Follow the path as it climbs, turns and drops again, eventually reaching a stile.
- Cross the stile and turn left for 20 yards. Just before a road, turn left and follow the path, with the road on the right through the trees. The path eventually becomes enclosed and drops to the road.
- Turn left down the road for 50 yards, then turn right at a footpath sign, up steps. Retrace your outward journey for 250 yards, keeping the wall on your left, to reach the Kings Arms and the car park entrance again.

# Deal: Tudor castles and 18th-century port

**Distance:** 8 miles
**Map:** OS sheet 179
**Start and Parking:** The walk starts from the entrance to Deal pier (grid ref: 378528). There is plentiful parking along the seafront, north of the pier, and some street parking near the castle. There are also pay and display car parks in the town itself.
**Refreshments:** Public houses, shops and cafés in Deal.

### Historical Background

From the 17th until the middle of the 19th century, Deal was one of England's major seaports, despite having neither harbour nor docks. Three miles out to sea are the notorious Goodwin Sands, a vast sandbank lying for most of the time just below the surface of the water, responsible for wrecking countless vessels and claiming more than 50,000 lives in the past three centuries. The water between the Goodwin Sands and the shore, called the Downs, is sheltered by the sandbank and is one of the largest safe anchorages around Britain's coastline. In times of war merchant ships would creep down the coasts to congregate in the Downs, waiting to form up into huge convoys, often of many hundreds of ships, before setting sail across the world. Royal Navy fleets of warships and transports would also wait in the Downs for departure. Deal grew to pre-eminence as a town for supplying the needs of these convoys and fleets, and as a terminus for travellers and mail joining the ships.

Smuggling began in earnest all along the south coast in the 17th century. Proximity to France and wide open beaches made Deal a smugglers' paradise, and smuggling was a major part of the local economy. Spirits, tobacco, tea, silk and fancy goods crossed the channel at night in the famous 'Deal Galleys', boats with false keels and hollow masts for the hiding of contraband. Much of the town was involved in, or turned a blind eye to, smuggling, and many members of the aristocracy or the wealthy classes would travel to Deal to openly buy smuggled merchandise. Consequently, it was extremely difficult for customs officers to gain sufficient public support to suppress this activity. After 1816, stern measures were taken to suppress smuggling: the Coastal Blockade was started, and after many violent confrontations the trade was finally stamped out by the middle of the 1850s.

However, as well as being a major point of departure from Britain, the flat beaches and safe anchorage around Deal made the area a major danger spot at times when invasion by a continental enemy threatened. To counter one such threat, Henry VIII built three massive castles – Walmer, Deal and Sandown – to defend the beaches. These castles

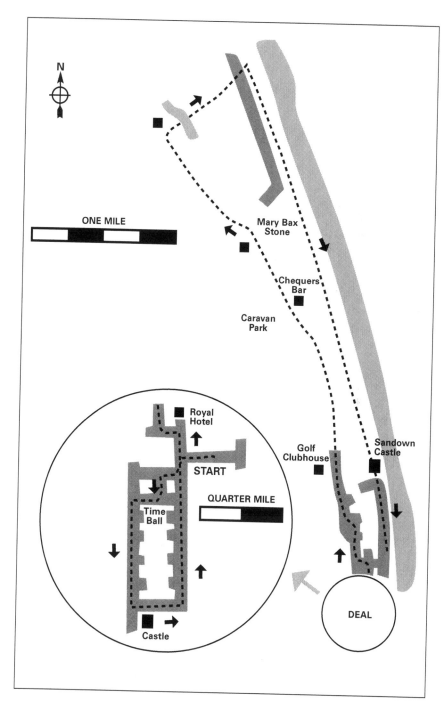

again saw service during the Napoleonic Wars, when the Downs were used as a springboard from which the English fleet and expeditionary forces could attack the French.

### The Walk
This walk goes through historic Deal and passes many sites from its heyday in the Napoleonic era, and then rambles through links and dunes before returning along the coast. The walk also encompasses two of Henry VIII's great fortifications, and the landing site of Caesar's second expedition in 54BC.

● With your back to the pier entrance, cross the road and turn left.
● Cross Broad Street and turn down it for 20 yards, and then turn left into Middle Street.
● At the end of Middle Street, turn right down the broad South Street.

*South Street was always the terminus for public transport coming into Deal. During the 18th and 19th centuries horse-drawn coaches used to arrive and depart from South Street, connecting Deal with destinations across all of England. Passengers sailing from England would travel to Deal and stay in one of its numerous inns until their fleet was ready to sail. Navy captains would also often join their ships here rather than sailing down the coast with their vessel, travelling overland and staying in comfort onshore until it was time to depart.*

The entrance to Deal Castle, one of the finest examples of military building from the reign of Henry VIII.

- At the bottom of South Street, turn left. Shortly cross Sondes Road and keep straight on.
- Keep to the left-hand side of the road and cross over four side roads to reach Deal Castle.

*Henry VIII's foreign and domestic policies culminated in the break from the Church of Rome in 1534. This resulted in war and made invasion by the leading Catholic powers, headed by France, seem likely. The coastline around Deal was fortified by three huge castles. These were state-of-the-art military architecture. For mediaeval castles, assault had been by foot soldiers backed by primitive siege weapons, and therefore high thick walls were all important. But by the 16th century gunpowder had revolutionised siege warfare, and assault would now be backed by efficient cannon. Castles had to be redesigned to cope with this new threat.*

*Deal is a classic example of Henrician military architecture, comparatively low and squat but with thick rounded walls to deflect cannon ball, flat gun platforms which would give visibility over as great an arc as possible and which could provide fields of interlocking cannon fire, and a dry moat which could be riddled by musket fire from commanding windows and turned into an effective killing field.*

*Deal Castle has six huge semi-circular bastions, surmounted by a further six smaller bastions, providing a 360 degree field of fire. It had an oven for heating cannon balls, and cunningly placed sally ports which enabled the defender to launch an attack on any assailants from the rear. Deal would normally have had a defence force of a captain and 24 men (although in times of trouble many more could be accommodated), and the captain of Deal Castle also had responsibility for the nearby garrisons in Walmer and Sandown Castles.*

*The only time Deal Castle saw any fighting was during the Civil War, when the castles were held for the king and besieged in 1648 by parliamentary forces. Major-General Gibson held Deal for some weeks against an attacking force of 2,000 men before finally surrendering.*

**Deal Castle is open from 1 April to 30 September daily, 10am–6pm. There is an admission charge, but it is free to English Heritage members.**

- Walk past the castle onto the seafront. Turn left along the sea front towards the pier. In 200 yards pass the time ball on your left.

*The tower, which is now crowned by a time ball, stood at the main entrance to the Naval Yard in Deal. The Naval Yard was built in the late 18th century to provide Royal Navy vessels anchored in the Downs with a governmental victualling yard rather than relying on the free enterprise of the town.*

*The tower was built in 1795–96 as a signalling tower, as one of a series, each one within sight of the next in line, stretching from Deal to London, with the purpose of alerting the government to any impending invasion by the French. The tower originally housed a shutter semaphore, which passed signals by means of huge wooden shutters in front of a lamp to the next tower along the line. A signal could be transmitted from Deal to the Admiralty in London in under two minutes. In 1816 the semaphore was replaced by two huge arms on a pole as a more effective means of communication, but this fell into disuse in 1842.*

*In 1853 the present time ball was installed, as the tower was put to the new use of receiving a time signal from Greenwich Observatory transmitted down the line of towers to ports around the coast. At 12.55 the ball was raised to the top of the mast, and at 1pm precisely the ball dropped, providing an accurate visual time signal against which all the ships anchored in the Downs could set their timepieces. The time ball was used until 1927, when the invention of radio rendered it obsolete.*

**The Tower now houses a small museum and is open May to September, 10am–5pm, except Mondays.**

- Pass the pier and continue along the seafront for another 100 yards, as far as the Royal Hotel.

*The Royal Hotel was the most prestigious hotel in Deal, used by many famous personages awaiting the arrival of the fleet or waiting for their ship to be ready for departure. Horatio Nelson often stayed in the Royal, accompanied in later years by his mistress Emma Hamilton.*

- Cross the road in front of the Royal Hotel and turn left down King Street. Take the first road on the right, Middle Street, and follow it as it winds parallel to the seafront, ignoring all side turns.

*Middle Street is the oldest part of Deal and was once the main road in the town. It grew to prosperity in the 1600s, with the influx of many Flemish refugees. It contains buildings from many eras, and some of its present buildings date from the early 18th century.*

*Deal had a reputation for being a very rough town, combining all the worst excesses of a port with the lawlessness associated with being a smugglers haunt. In 1710 it was described as being 'an impious and remorseless town: fraud, oppression, theft and rapine reign'. Middle Street and the maze of courts and narrow alleys running of it was at the insalubrious heart of Deal, teaming with smugglers, press gangs, brothels and inns.*

*During the Napoleonic Wars, the smugglers were tolerated as they provided a valuable source of information about what was happening on the Continent as well as bringing goods to England through the French blockade.*

- Eventually reach Alfred Square.

*The Prince Albert public house, on the corner of Middle Street, was built in 1717. At one time its landlord, William Riley, was strongly suspected of being the leader of the Deal smuggling community, although this was never proven and he was never brought to justice.*

- Turn left down Alfred Square, and at the bottom turn right (College Road).

*The road you are turning into is called College Road. Its continuation southwards is called High Street. Up until around 1600, this road marked the old shoreline: gradually a shingle beach was laid down by the sea, where the current shoreline now is, and a brackish marsh formed between beach and shore. Over the next century this marsh was reclaimed and the land used for the expanding town of Deal. High Street is so-called not because it was the main street of the town but because it once marked the limit of the high tides.*

- Follow College Road for nearly half a mile, passing from the old town into newer housing. Cross Harold Road and keep straight on, now up King Edward Road.
- At a T-junction turn left into Godwyn Road.
- At the bottom of Godwyn Road, turn right into Golf Road.
- Follow Golf Road, ignoring side turns as it becomes a no through road and passes a Southern Water Treatment Plant on the right.
- Keep straight on up the road, with a golf course on the right, soon passing the golf club house on the left.
- At the end of the tarmacked road do not turn into the entrance of Leisurescope Caravan Park but keep straight on along a sandy trackway, with golf links to your right.
- After half a mile pass a pillbox on your right and keep ahead along the track.

*This World War Two pillbox is a reminder that the threat of invasion onto this flat and accessible coast was not confined to Tudor or Napoleonic times. This whole coastline was heavily fortified with mines and barbed wire backed by fortified gun emplacements.*

- The track ends at the Chequers Bar. Join the road and maintain the same direction, passing the entrance to the caravan park on your left.

*You are following an ancient trackway that threaded its way through the dunes just above what used to be the high-water mark before the sea wall was built. It was used by smugglers to move their wares between Deal and Sandwich while avoiding the main road, which was likely to be patrolled by excise men.*

- Turn left with the road, avoiding a track straight ahead marked with a 'Private Property' sign. The right of way now no longer follows the road but runs along the top of a bank about 30 yards to the left. This is at first overgrown, but soon becomes a clear pathway, with good views over the fens to the left.
- Just before a cottage, pass the Mary Bax Stone, set on the right of the bank.

*This stone marks the spot where Mary Bax, a local woman, was murdered in 1782 by a foreign seaman.*

- Cross the drive to the cottage and cross a stile opposite to continue along the top of the bank.
- In 100 yards, where the bank turns away to the right, keep straight on to a stile by a field gate.
- Go over the stile and maintain the same line of advance, with the fence on your left.
- At the end of the field, go through the gate and continue ahead, still with the fence on the left.
- Cross the stile and maintain the same line of advance through a third field, still following the fence on your left.
- Pass a pumping station off to your right, and then cross into the next field. At the time of writing there was no stile at this point, but keep straight on, still with the fence on your left.
- At the end of the field, cross a stile into a farm drive and turn right. Follow the drive, passing the farm on your left, and continue to the road.
- Cross the road and cross a stile opposite and enter a field.
- Cross the field to a stile on the opposite side. Cross the stile to enter rough pasture.
- Keep straight on, following a series of concrete marker posts, to a stile onto the golf course.
- Continue across the golf course, following concrete markers, and soon bear right with the now wider path, and then curve left again.
- Cross a stile onto the coast road and turn right.
- Pass in front of houses and continue along the coast road.

*Somewhere along this stretch of coastline, between Sandwich and Sandown Castle (no one knows exactly where), is the site of Julius Caesar's second landing in Britain, in 54BC. Caesar had made a brief reconnaissance the previous year, landing four miles south of here, near modern Walmer, but the expedition had been pinned to its beachhead and forced to evacuate. In 54BC Caesar returned, this time earlier in the year and with a far larger force. He conducted a vigorous campaign, thrusting up through Kent and across the Thames, fighting a series of skirmishes against British guerrillas before defeating his main opponent Cassivellaunus at Wheathampstead in Hertfordshire. The Romans then withdrew from Britain for nearly a century, until returning to launch a full-blown invasion, landing five miles north of here, at Richborough, in AD43 (see walk 4).*

- Where the houses end and the road turns right, keep straight on along the sea wall at the top of pebble beach.
- Follow the sea wall for one and three quarter miles. The footpath is now officially below the sea wall on the right, along the edge of the golf course. This is softer walking but loses the view of the sea. It is suggested you take either the sea wall or the footpath, or alternate between the two, whichever you prefer.
- Eventually reach houses and a road. Turn left onto the promenade.

*The circular bastion at the end of the promenade marks the site of Sandown Castle.*

*Built in 1539–40 as the third of Henry VIII's 'Castles of the Downs', Sandown was smaller than Deal or Walmer, having only four semi-circular batteries rather than six. It was under the command of the captain of Deal Castle.*

*Sandown Castle never saw action in Henry's day, but during the Civil War was held by royalist troops for three months. After the end of the Civil War, it was used as a prison for Colonel Hutchinson, one of the signatories to Charles I's death warrant, who languished in its damp vaults for a year before dying of pneumonia.*

*During the 18th century the castle was abandoned and much damaged by the encroaching sea. It was regarrisoned during the invasion scare of 1803–07, but was finally abandoned in 1815 and allowed to crumble away.*

● Keep along the promenade until you reach the pier.

*The road along the promenade is Beach Street. As Deal had no harbour, in the 18th and 19th centuries this was the boatman's area of Deal, with boats running straight on and off the beach. Not only did fishing boats land here, but ferries carried passengers from the inns of the town and victuals from the port out to the waiting ships. All of the trades that supported a fleet getting ready for sea – rope and sail making, boat building, bakeries, breweries etc – were clustered along Beach Street, as well as provisioners for meat, fruit and vegetables.*

# WALK 22
# Hythe and the Napoleonic Wars

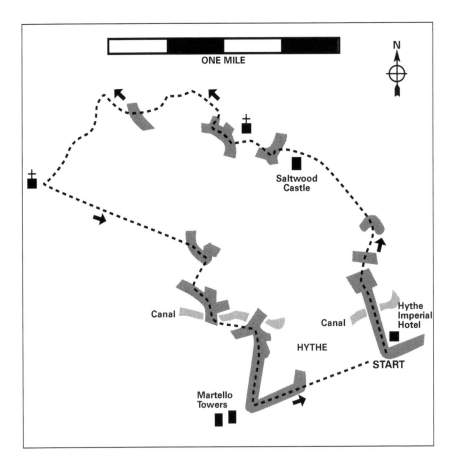

**Distance:** 5.5 miles

**Map:** OS sheet 179 or 189

**Start and Parking:** The walk starts from the Hythe Imperial Hotel, on Princes Parade, which is part of Hythe seafront (grid ref:168344). There is a car park opposite the hotel, or street parking along Princes Parade.

**Refreshments.** Public houses, shops and tearooms in Hythe.

## Historical Background

In 1802 the Peace Treaty of Amiens ended nine years of war between Britain and revolutionary France. This was only a temporary respite, for 14 months later the war resumed. This time France was led by a far more formidable enemy, Napoleon Bonaparte, whose primary war aim for the next two years was the invasion of England.

Napoleon's obvious invasion route was the short sea crossing from the Pas de Calais to the beaches of Kent, in particular the coast between the cliffs of Hastings in the west and Folkestone in the east. Here wide beaches were backed by the flat fields of the Romney marshes, ideal countryside for the highly-manoeuvrable French army. Although the first line of defence was the English Navy, there was always the danger that the French fleet would manage to secure the channel for 24 hours, all the time that would be necessary for an invasion armada to hand Napoleon's Grande Armee on England's shores. Protection for many miles of exposed beaches became of paramount importance, with only limited funds available for the task.

The solution was the Martello Tower, a string of brick-built gun-platform-cum-watch towers built in close proximity to each other all along the coast, providing mutual reinforcement and interlocking fields of fire. No single tower was strong enough to withstand prolonged naval bombardment, but they could repel assault by infantry, and their sheer numbers would ensure devastating firepower against any landing force.

However, if an invasion force did manage to suppress the beach defences and get ashore, a fallback line of defence was required to stop the French spilling rapidly across the Romney Marshes. This was provided by the Royal Military Canal, effectively a moat running along the inland edge of the marsh. The great strength of the Napoleonic army was its ability to combine the three wings of infantry, cavalry and artillery into one devastating combined attack. The canal was built to combat this strength, by providing a barrier which would break up any combined attack trying to cross under fire. It would stop cavalry and artillery from crossing and any infantry who swam the canal would not arrive on the far side with dry powder, and thus fall easy prey to the waiting British.

## The Walk

**This walk goes through the hilly countryside above Hythe and passes mediaeval Saltwood Castle. It returns through Hythe, going along part of the Royal Military Canal, and visiting two Martello Towers.**

- From the car park, and facing the Hythe Imperial Hotel, walk directly away from the sea, down the road to the left of the hotel, signed Town Centre. Cross over South Street and Fisher Close, and quarter of a mile from the seafront, cross over the Royal Military Canal.
- Continue on to the main road. Cross the road and keep straight ahead, to the left of the Bell public house.

*This main road was the shoreline in the Middle Ages, when Hythe was an important port. The name Hythe is old english for harbour, which crops up in other ports e.g. along the Thames as part of Greenhithe.*

*Hythe was one of the original Cinque Ports, a group of ports along the English Channel which were granted special privileges by the Crown in return for supplying ships to them in time of war. (Before the time of Henry VIII there was no Royal Navy: when ships were needed to fight at sea or for transport duties private vessels were hired by the king.) The importance of Hythe is reflected in the fact that the town sent 11 ships to fight against the Spanish Armada in 1588, an unusually large contingent.*

- After 50 yards cross a quiet back lane and go straight on up Mill Lane, soon a footpath, passing an old converted mill on your left.
- At the top of the footpath climb some steps up to a road. Cross the road and continue straight on down an enclosed footpath.
- After 350 yards turn right with the footpath and climb some concrete steps to emerge onto a drive.
- Turn left past the gate to Saltwood Lodge and walk down the track. After 40 yards do not turn left with the track but cross the stile ahead.
- Continue ahead along the top of a field, with fence, trees and disused railway embankment on your right.

*The railway line was built at the end of the era of 19th-century railway mania, when branch lines were being constructed to any conceivable destinations. This line connected Sandling on the main line to Sandgate on the coast, to bring holidaymakers onto the coast. The plan was to extend the line to Folkestone, but it had proved economically unviable before the work was completed. The Sandling–Sandgate link was closed as a result of the Beeching cuts of the 1960s.*

- Follow the fenced embankment down to a gate and stile.
- Cross the stile and keep straight on along a track, still following the embankment. The track is soon fenced and leads to a metal gate.
- Pass through the gate and keep ahead along the track, soon passing the walls of Saltwood Castle on your left.

*Saltwood has been fortified since the time of the Romans. In those days Saltwood was on the coast and a fortified port, standing just off Stane Street, the Roman arterial road running from Lympne and linking a series of minor channel coast ports to Canterbury. In AD488 Aesc, son of the legendary Saxon warlord Hengist, built a fort here to protect the harbour, one of a string of fortifications along the so-called Saxon Shore.*

*The present castle was built in the 12th century by Henry de Essex, standard-bearer to Henry II and Warden of the Cinque Ports, of which Hythe was one. It was jointly owned by de Essex and the Archbishop of Canterbury, Thomas Becket. When de Essex was disgraced for cowardice, his share of the castle reverted to the Crown. Becket demanded that total control of the castle be given to him, but Henry II appointed the Sheriff of Kent, Randolph de Broc, as constable. De Broc was later excommunicated by Becket for seizing church land, and became the Archbishop's bitter enemy. In December 1170 de Broc offered shelter to four knights newly arrived from France and en route to Canterbury to carry out King Henry's instructions to murder Becket (see walk 7). Afterwards they stayed at Saltwood again before departing to France to report the success of their mission to the king.*

*The castle remained jointly owned by the Archbishopric of Canterbury and the Crown until 1540, when Archbishop Cranmer gave it to Henry VIII. In 1580 an earthquake rendered the castle uninhabitable, until it was restored in the 19th century by the Deedes family. Later the castle was owned by the historian Sir Kenneth Clarke and then his son, Alan Clark MP.*

- Follow the track, soon broad and tree lined, around the moat and curtain wall of the castle and out to a road.
- Turn left along the road and follow it around a bend. Ignore a side turn. At the end of the farm yard on the right, and opposite some houses, turn right into a footpath along the farm boundary.
- At the end of the enclosed footpath go through a kissing gate and turn half-left across a field to a gate into the churchyard.
- Follow the path through the churchyard and exit via a lychgate. Follow the path to a road.
- Turn right along the road. In 30 yards ignore a footpath on the right, but in another 30 yards turn right down a no through road.
- Where the road bends right, keep ahead up a bridleway that initially runs alongside the road but soon climbs away, passing orchards on the left.
- Descend with the path to cross the top of a track coming in from the right. Keep ahead up the bridleway and in 100 yards turn left over a stile.
- Immediately over the stile, fork right and follow a path uphill.
- After 100 yards, at a cross track, turn left downhill, keeping the fence on the right, to eventually cross a stile.
- Continue ahead on a clear path through open scrubland. The path soon becomes enclosed and descends to cross a footbridge onto a road.
- Turn half-left across the road to a kissing gate. Follow the footpath (Saxon Shore Way) along the right-hand edge of a field and through a gate into woods.

*In Roman and Saxon times the shoreline was considerably further inland than at present. Over the centuries the coastline has receded, leaving former ports such as Saltwood and Lympne stranded inland, and leading to the development of new ports such as Hythe on the new coastline. Now the port of Hythe has itself been cut off from the sea by the shingle beach that is followed by the present promenade. The Saxon Shore Way is a long-distance path following the course of the coastline as it was in the Dark Ages.*

- Descend through the woods, but in 100 yards, just before a gate, turn left and descend through trees to cross a footbridge.
- Continue along the footpath through the woods. In a quarter of a mile ignore a turning to the right but keep straight on up a grassy track. Soon swing left up a slope into trees and to a gate to enter a field.
- To cross this field you must use two rights of way which are not, however, the most direct line. From the gate, cross half-right, aiming at the church and house seen opposite.
- Cross a stile, turn left for 15 yards past the rear of the church, then turn left through a gate back into the field you have just left.
- Follow the fence on the right. Ignore a stile on the right after 100 yards and continue down the fence to gates at the bottom right corner. Pass through the pedestrian gate beside the metal field gate.
- Continue ahead with a fence on your right. At the end of the fence, go half-left across the field to a gate seen in the distance.
- Go through the gate and along a fenced footpath down the edge of a wood. Follow the path as it drops, soon with a field on the left.
- Ignore two stiles on the left, but descend and swing right to cross a footbridge.
- Continue along the path, bearing left to continue ahead with a fence on the right.
- Ignore a kissing gate on the left and keep straight on, soon ignoring a turning on the right.
- At a T-junction, turn right and follow the track as it swings around to the left and eventually comes out at the head of a tarmacked road.
- Cross over the end of the road and turn right down a footpath, passing between garden fences to reach a road.
- Turn left down the road. In 150 yards cross Barrack Hill and bend right with the road to reach traffic lights.
- Cross Military Road at the lights. Keep straight on to cross a bridge over the canal, with the entrance to the Hythe and Dymchurch Light Railway on the opposite side of the road.
- Immediately over the bridge, turn left onto a path along the edge of the canal.

*The Royal Military Canal was constructed on the orders of Prime Minister Pitt the Younger in 1803, when the fears of invasion by Napoleon were at their height. This was a deep channel running for 23 miles along the inland edge of Romney Marsh, to provide a fall-back line of defence should the French manage to gain a beachhead.*

*The canal was built to break up any combined assault by Napoleon's Grande Armee, by providing a deep ditch running in a series of zigzags, thus allowing a deadly cross-fire from the gun emplacements built every quarter of a mile along the far side. As a further defence, sluice gates were built into the canal to allow the low-lying Romney Marsh to be flooded if necessary, thereby further disrupting an invaders advance. The canal was finished in 1809, but by that time the threat of invasion had receded and it was never used.*

- Follow the canal bank. Ignore a footbridge and keep ahead, until the path swings to join the road and the canal passes under a road bridge.
- Cross half-left over the road and resume the walk along the canal bank, still with the canal on your left.
- Two hundred yards past the road bridge, turn up the first road on the right, St Leonard's Road, passing Waterside Court and a school on your left.
- At a road junction keep ahead up St Leonard's Road to reach the seafront.
- The Martello Towers are along the beach to your right. To view them more closely, descend onto the pebble beach and turn right. Walk past fishing boats and fishermen's sheds to the Martello Towers.

*In 1804–05 a line of towers were built along the shoreline of England, most of them along the coast from Portsmouth to Folkestone. These were called Martello Towers, named after a*

Martello Towers on the beach at Hythe, built to withstand the threat of invasion by Napoleon.

*stone-built tower at Mortella on Corsica. Circular fortified towers had fallen out of fashion by the 16th century, when the invention of gunpowder made them vulnerable to bombardment, but when Mortella Tower had been occupied by pirates and held out for two days against the Royal Navy, this wisdom was reassessed.*

*Each Martello Tower had the same design. They were 33 feet tall, with walls between 13 feet wide at the base to 6 feet wide at parapet level, and slightly elliptical in shape, with the thickest part of the walls seaward. They were built of brick and strengthened with lime mortar to withstand bombardment. Entrance was at first-floor level, on the landward side, and there was room for a garrison of 24 men and one officer to be rapidly posted into each tower when required, with slit windows to enable the beach to be raked with musket fire. On the flat roof of each tower was a gun capable of traversing 360 degrees. This could fire either a 24-pound cannon ball 1,000 yards, which would have caused immense damage to lightly-built landing craft approaching the beaches, or it could fire grape-shot, a canister which would spray between 84 and 232 musket balls up to 350 yards, with devastating effect upon infantry. Where the threat was greatest, as here at Hythe, the towers were built to be 700 yards apart, so that they could command the whole beach with interlocking cannon fire.*

*The towers were cheap and quick to build, and in total 103 were built at the instruction of Prime Minister Pitt the Younger. The destruction of the French and Spanish navies at Trafalgar in 1805 removed the threat of invasion and the towers never saw active service. Many were allowed to fall into disrepair during the 19th century, and some were used for naval target practice and destroyed. In 1940 the surviving towers were repaired and put on a war footing again in the face of threatened German invasion.*

*The towers at Hythe are good examples of Martello Towers and clearly show how their interlocking fields of fire would have operated. Six miles down the coast, at Dymchurch, there is a fully-restored tower which is well worth visiting. Open weekends March to July 12–4pm, daily during August 12–4pm. There is an admission charge, but it is free to English Heritage Members.*

● Retrace your steps to the promenade and keep ahead along it for three quarters of a mile to return to the car park.

*The fifth house you pass, 100 yards along the promenade, is a converted Martello Tower.*

WALK 23

# Westerham:
# Wolfe and Churchill

**Distance:** 5 miles
**Map:** OS sheet 187 and OS sheet 188
**Start and Parking:** The walk starts from the centre of Westerham (grid ref: 447541). Westerham is situated on the A25, five miles west of Sevenoaks. Although there are several car parks and limited street parking in Westerham, it is recommended that you park in the pay and display car park, on the north side of the A25, just on the eastern edge of Westerham.
**Refreshments:** Public houses and tearooms in Westerham.

### Historical Background

Westerham is the most westerly village in Kent (its name comes from the Anglo-Saxon for western 'Ham' or settlement), and there has been a settlement here or nearby since the Iron Age. Although very picturesque in its own right, its main claim to fame is its association with two of Britain's most famous heroes, General James Wolfe and Sir Winston Churchill.

James Wolfe was born in Westerham in 1727 into a military family. He gained his commission in the army at the age of 14 (not especially young for the 18th century), fought with distinction at the Battle of Culloden, and rose to be England's youngest-ever Major General at the age of 30. In 1759 he was given command of the expeditionary force sent to dislodge the French from Canada. After an inconclusive winter campaign up and down the St Lawrence River, Wolfe retrieved the situation by a brilliant but risky assault upon Quebec in March 1759. Through a combination of an audacious night time ascent of the Heights of Abraham and poor French generalship, Wolfe won the battle which made Canada British, but he lost his life in the process.

Winston Churchill's early career was brilliant if also chequered. A soldier and a war correspondent, Churchill entered parliament as a Conservative in 1900 but swapped to the Liberal party in 1904 He held a succession of cabinet offices until 1921 and was involved in a number of controversial political decisions. With the fall of Lloyd George in 1922, Churchill lost both office and seat. He returned to parliament in 1924, this time as a Conservative again, but he was not trusted by party or public, and in 1929 he went into a political wilderness, from which he emerged in 1940 to become one of Britain's greatest-ever wartime leaders. Although rejected by the electorate in 1945, Churchill became Prime Minister again in 1951, before finally retiring four years later.

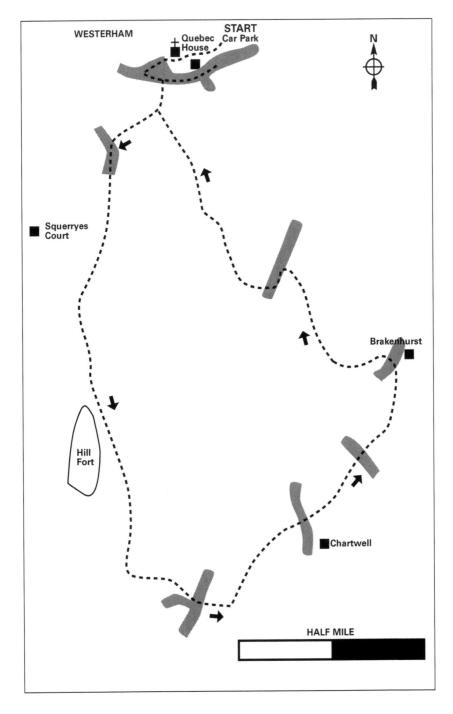

The period of Churchill's political exile in the 20s and 30s, and most of his post-war years were spent at his home at Chartwell near Westerham, where he did much of his writing and painting.

**The Walk**
**This walk goes through rolling and wooded countryside on the Greensand Ridge, passing the original Iron Age settlement in the area and going past both Chartwell and Wolfe's childhood home, Quebec House.**

● From the car park, follow the clearly-marked footpath that runs parallel with the main A25 back into the village. Pass through the churchyard and onto the village green.

*The Church of St Mary the Virgin is partly 13th century, with the low tower and short spire common to many churches in Kent, and with 19th-century restorations. It has a 14th-century spiral staircase leading to the tower and the coat of arms of Edward VI, the only examples of either found in a Kentish church. There is also a memorial stone to General Wolfe. His body lies in St Alfege's Church in Greenwich.*

*On the green are statues of Westerham's two famous heroes: a modern bronze statue of Sir Winston Churchill, by sculptor Oscar Nemon, and an older statue of an earlier hero, General James Wolfe.*

The village green at Westerham.

- Standing on the green, with your back to the statue of Churchill, cross the main A25 to a footpath, signposted up a short flight of steps and called Water Lane.
- Descend the enclosed footpath, crossing two small streams, to reach a swing gate leading into a meadow.
- Pass through the swing gate and turn right, following a path with a hedge and stream on your right and a slope initially on your left.
- Follow the path to a swing gate beside a footbridge. Go through the gate onto a lane and turn left to cross the bridge.
- Follow the rough track to reach a half-timbered house. Proceed to the left corner of the house, where there are two stiles. Cross the rightmost stile (marked Greensand Way Link Path) onto an enclosed track.
- Follow the enclosed path up the slope to a stile.

*Looking back and to the left there is a view of Squerryes Court nestling in the trees below. This is a fine William & Mary mansion built in 1681 and it was the home of the Warde family from 1731, who built up the fine collection of Dutch Old Masters on view today. The young James Wolfe, who lived nearby in what is now called Quebec House, was a friend of the family and often visited Squerryes Court.*

**Squerryes Court is privately occupied but open to the public on occasions.**

- Cross the stile and continue along the enclosed path across Squerryes Park.
- At the end of the enclosed path, continue straight on, aiming for a stile in the middle of a band of trees seen ahead.
- Cross this stile, pass through trees and continue straight on to another stile heading onto a farm track.
- Turn left onto this track and follow it as it descends into the valley bottom.
- At a T-junction in the valley bottom, keep straight on for 100 yards to reach a stile at the corner of a wood.

*In the woods is an old Iron Age hillfort. The ramparts of its northern perimeter can just be seen if you look carefully to the right, just beyond the fence. This fort was quite small, only 400 yards long by 100 yards at its widest, with a single rampart and ditch.*

- Cross the stile and continue straight on, with the wood and fort on your right and the valley dropping away to the left.
- Cross a stile and continue straight on, soon on a clear track across more level ground, leaving the wood and a distinctive white house away to your right. Continue straight on to a stile seen ahead, leading into woods.
- Cross the stile and take the middle of three tracks, the most straight one of the three, climbing steeply up through woods and rhododendrons.
- Pass over a cross track and continue straight on. The path soon levels out, and then climbs again, more gently this time, to reach a T-junction.

- Turn left onto an initially broader path.
- After 250 yards, at a fork, take the left fork and descend steeply.
- Join another path and continue to descend.
- At the bottom of the slope, turn briefly right to reach a drive to a house. Do not turn into the drive gates but turn left and follow the drive up to a road.
- Cross the road onto a bridle path and climb steeply.
- At the top of the slope, where a path joins from the right, keep straight on with a fence on your right, for 50 yards to a fork. Here turn left, following the Greensand Way.
- In 250 yards, at a fork, take the right fork, maintaining a generally forward direction The path is still signed Greensand Way.
- Descend through coppiced woodland, ignoring all side turns. The path descends ever more steeply, until finally steps are reached down onto a road.
- Cross the road to a footpath opposite, labelled 'French Street', just to left of gates to Chartwell.

*There has been a building on the site of Chartwell since 1350, although only a modest farmhouse for many centuries. It was enlarged as a Victorian country mansion in the middle of the 19th century, and is surrounded by 800 acres of grounds. It was bought by Churchill in 1922 and was his home for the next 40 years. Its park and setting appealed immediately to Churchill the painter, and he saw in its grounds and gardens the tranquillity necessary for writing. He extensively redesigned the house and had much of it rebuilt, and in the grounds he indulged in another hobby, bricklaying: many of the walls in the gardens were built by Churchill for recreation.*

*The purchase of Chartwell followed Churchill's loss of government office and a parliamentary seat in 1922. He returned to parliament in 1924 and also returned to the government under Stanley Baldwin for the next five years. But in 1929 Churchill lost office and was in the political wilderness until 1939. During that time Churchill called Chartwell an 'oasis in his political desert' and devoted himself to personal interests – writing, painting, bricklaying and his family. It was here that he wrote his* History of the English Speaking Peoples.

*Chartwell was closed for the war: it was too close to the channel coast and the threatened invasion of Kent to be a safe residence for the Prime Minister, which he had become in 1940, and its lakes made it an easily-identifiable target from the air. When Churchill fell from office in 1945 he again retired to Chartwell, which remained his home for the rest of his life.*

*The house is a fascinating museum to Churchill the private man rather than the public figure. The museum room contains gifts given to him by international figures during a career spanning half a century, a collection of his more exotic clothes and memorabilia of his life, including the Boer War 'Wanted Dead or Alive' poster of Churchill. The rest of the house reflects the many facets of his life, and includes his study, his writing desk and his easels.*

**Chartwell is open from March to the end of October, Wednesday to Sunday, 11am–5.00pm. There is an admission charge, but it is free to National Trust members.**

Winston Churchill, whose statue stands on Westerham village green, made Chartwell his home from 1922 onwards.

- Climb the enclosed footpath for a quarter of a mile to reach a road at the top of the slope. Cross the road and go through a gate opposite.
- Keep straight on down a bridle path, soon descending.
- After 250 yards, keep right at a fork (still signed Greensand Way).

*Across the valley to the right is a view of distinctive Kentish oasthouses. Oasthouses were designed to store and dry hops. This one, at Outridge farm, is square, which was the original shape for them throughout the country. Hop farmers in Kent decided that oasthouses would be more efficient if they were round, thereby avoiding corners in which undried hops could accumulate. In fact, round was no more efficient than square as a shape, and the design was discontinued, but not before the round oasthouse had become the fixed image of what one should look like.*

- Four hundred yards later, bear left at a fork and 50 yards further on emerge onto a tarmacked drive.
- Turn right up the drive for 50 yards, then turn left onto a footpath, just before the gates to Brackenhurst.
- Keep straight on along the path through the woods.
- At a T-junction, turn left up a waymarked path. Keep straight on for 300 yards, ignoring tracks to left and right and crossing a cross track.
- When a deeply rutted tractor track is reached, turn left for 30 yards and then turn right again to continue the same line of advance along a waymarked footpath. The path soon widens.
- Follow the footpath to eventually emerge at a car park.
- Follow the left-hand edge of the car park to the road. Cross the road and turn left for 40 yards, before turning half-right onto a footpath. This path is initially narrow and overgrown and starts off parallel to the road, but soon veers away from it.
- At a T-junction with a broader track, turn right and descend for 200 yards to reach wooden posts.
- Pass through the wooden posts, turn right and descend the track.
- After 300 yards, turn right at a T-junction. Continue to descend, with woods on your left and soon with a fenced driveway on your right, to reach a stile.
- Cross the stile and turn right sharply uphill.
- At the top of the slope, keep straight on. Soon the spire of Westerham Church is seen directly ahead. Keep straight on until the slope starts to descend, and then bear half-left on a clear path to a stile.
- Cross the stile and continue to descend, aiming to the right of tennis courts seen ahead to reach a swing gate.
- Pass through the swing gate and climb the enclosed path (Water Lane again) to reach Westerham village green.
- Cross the road to the green but instead of crossing the green back to the churchyard, turn right down the A25. In 300 yards you reach Quebec House on your left.

*In 1726 the Wolfe family moved into The Spires, as it was then called, and the following year James was born in the nearby Westerham Vicarage. James's father was an officer in the Marines and there was a long tradition of military service in the Wolfe family, which it was always assumed James would follow. Young James lived here for the first 12 years of his life until in 1739 his family moved to Greenwich, in order for James to attend the prestigious Westons Military College there.*

*The house is a Tudor brick building with a fine collection of gables, and was renamed Quebec House after Wolfe's death to commemorate his famous victory Although somewhat*

James Wolfe, hero of Quebec, lived at Quebec House in Westerham.

*altered in the intervening years, the basic house is still as it was when Wolfe lived there and today contains much memorabilia, especially paintings, statues and uniforms. The stable block has a display devoted to the Battle of Quebec.*

*The rather fine street wall of Quebec House was the inspiration for some of Winston Churchill's wall-building efforts in the gardens of Chartwell.*

**Quebec House is open from 1 April to the end of October, Wednesday to Sunday, 1–4.30pm. There is an admission charge, but it is free to National Trust members.**

● Continue for 100 yards along the A25 to reach the car park on your left.

# WALK 24
# Dover: White Cliffs and two World Wars

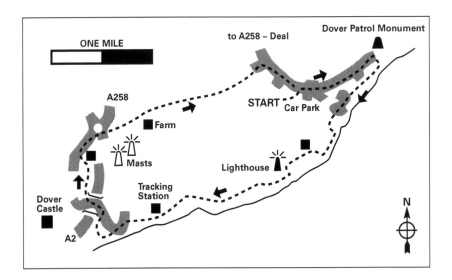

**Distance:** 8.5 miles

**Map:** OS sheet 179

**Start and Parking:** The walk starts from St Margaret's at Cliffe (grid ref: 359446). St Margaret's at Cliffe is four miles north of Dover and six miles south of Deal, at the end of a minor road signposted off the A258 Dover–Deal road. There is a free car park in the middle of the village.

**Refreshments:** Public houses, shops and a café at St Margaret's at Cliffe, café at the Dover Patrol monument.

### Historical Background

Dover, standing at the narrowest crossing point to the Continent, has always been the gateway into England for merchant, traveller and conqueror. It was the first point Julius Caesar made for in his reconnaissance raid of 55BC and William the Conqueror made it his target after defeating the English at Hastings. The massive fortifications built by the Normans have been added to over the centuries and the castle has remained garrisoned for 1,000 years, testimony to the castle's enduring importance to the nation's defences.

Dover saw its greatest wartime action during the two world wars of this century. Dover was the nerve-centre for the Royal Navy's Channel Command, and from here the Dover Patrol operated in 1914–18, keeping open the vital cross-channel link with the British forces fighting on the Western Front. In 1940, with the fall of France, the British Expeditionary Force of nearly a quarter of a million men, virtually the whole of Britain's fighting force, was left trapped in Belgium. The evacuation of this force from the beaches of Dunkirk was masterminded from operations rooms buried in the cliffs below Dover Castle.

Dover played a vital part in the defence of Britain during its time of greatest danger, the early years of World War Two. In the summer of 1940 Hitler decided upon Operation Sealion, the seaborne invasion of Britain. The prerequisite for this was the destruction of the RAF, in order that the invasion fleet could cross the channel unopposed. To achieve this, Reichmarshall Hermann Goring organised the Luftwaffe, the German airforce, for a sharp and decisive onslaught aimed at destroying Britain's aircraft and air fields. Radar defences installed along the clifftops provided the early warning system vital for the RAF to defend itself and the country.

**The Walk**

**This walk starts in St Margaret's at Cliffe and passes the Dover Patrol memorial. It then goes along the spectacular cliffs to Dover, passing many reminders of the action seen by this area in two world wars, and returns across rich agricultural land.**

- Leave the car park at St Margaret's at Cliffe via the access road. Return to the main road through the village and turn right.
- Pass the Hope Inn on the left and descend the main road. Follow the road as it curves left and ascends a hill.
- At the top of the rise, pass Lighthouse Road on the right and The Driveway on the left. Ten yards later, at a village green with a memorial, turn left into Granville Road.
- Follow Granville Road for half a mile. At a junction with Hotel Road on the right, and just after an unsuitable for long vehicles sign, keep straight on up Victoria Avenue.
- Keep straight on for 300 yards to reach the Dover Patrol monument.

*This monument was put up to commemorate the men who lost their lives in the Dover Patrol, a force of small ships that kept the channel open during World War One. A similar monument stands on the cliffs of Cap Blanc Nez on the opposite side of the English Channel, which are clearly visible on a fine day.*

*During the first decade of the 20th century, Britain had been involved in an arms race with Germany for naval supremacy. Resources had been poured into building battleships, cruisers and destroyers, and by the outbreak of World War One the Royal Navy had an immensely powerful surface fleet. However, the immediate problem in 1914 was to keep the vital supply route to France open, and to keep the English Channel clear of enemy mines. No provision had been made in pre-war planning for this essential task, and it was left to Admiral Hood, commander-in-chief at Dover, to improvise a defence force.*

Monument to the men who lost their lives on the Dover Patrol during World War One.

*Hood scratched together a hotchpotch of fishing boats and redundant naval vessels, unarmed apart from the occasional rife, manned mainly by local fishermen. In 1914 the Dover Patrol consisted of one yacht and four drifters; by the end of 1918 256 vessels had served in the patrol. This fragile flotilla served throughout the whole war, mainly clearing the mines that the Germans regularly scattered into the channel, occasionally having to protect shipping against German E-Boats (lightly armed fast motor boats) and submarines. On average each vessel swept 250 miles of sea each day for four years. In total 1,507 mines were destroyed. Over 2,000 men lost their lives doing this arduous and dangerous work. Thanks to the efforts of the Dover Patrol, the British Expeditionary Force was convoyed to France without mishap, and thereafter the supply route across the channel was kept open for four years with only very occasional interruptions.*

- After hooking at the monument, and perhaps visiting the café, retrace your steps back along the road for just a few yards. Just behind a National Trust sign, 'The Leas' on the left, turn left onto a vague footpath and descend through bushes.
- Follow the path to the cliff edge and turn right along the cliff. Eventually descend through trees. Nearly at the bottom of the slope, ignore steps on the left but follow the main path, soon with a fence on the left, out to a road.
- Turn left in the road and follow the road downhill.
- Immediately before the road bends sharply left and downhill, at a letter box, turn right up an unadopted drive, signposted 'Pine gardens and Museum'.

*Downhill this road leads to St Margaret's Bay, a peaceful little pebble-beached cove which is the traditional starting point for cross-channel swimmers.*

- In 30 yards fork left down Beach Road.
- Where the road ceases to be tarmacked, keep ahead up a rough track, passing houses on the left.
- At a cross track, turn left up a rough flinty track to reach a disused lighthouse on top of Lighthouse Down.
- Pass the lighthouse on your left to reach a footpath along the cliff top, and turn right along the cliffs.
- Walk along the cliffs. When a small wood bars your way, turn right and walk up to a track beside a cottage. Turn left along the track, now with the wood between you and the cliff edge.
- The track eventually bends right. Just after the bend, at a junction of tracks, turn left and follow the track to the gates of a lighthouse.

*These 400-foot high cliffs stand at the narrowest part of the English Channel. Three miles out to sea are the Goodwin Sands, a vast sandbank, most of the time just submerged and therefore an invisible but lethal danger to passing ships. Over the last 300 years over 50,000 lives have been lost by vessels being wrecked. To counter this hazard there has been a light on St Margaret's Cliffs since at least the Middle Ages, to warn sailors of the location of the sands.*

*Initially it was a beacon fire, manned intermittently by monks. Charles I granted permission for a permanent lighthouse to be built.*

- Turn left on a track, with the lighthouse on your right. Do not enter the gates of the keepers cottage, but keep ahead down an enclosed footpath between the cottage and the lighthouse.
- Follow the path to the cliff edge and turn right.

*Dover harbour is now in sight ahead.*

- Follow the path along the cliffs for one and a half miles. Keep to the upper path where there is a choice.

*You are walking along the famous White Cliffs of Dover, immortalised as an evocative image of peace in Vera Lynn's famous wartime song, and now green and tranquil. During World War Two this stretch of cliff was very different. Heavy guns were mounted on these cliffs, not only to command the Straits of Dover and deny passage to enemy shipping, but also heavy enough and with a long enough range to bombard enemy occupied France, 22 miles away. Although the guns have long since been removed, the concrete platforms upon which these huge guns stood can still be seen among the grass at intervals along the cliffs between here and Dover.*

- After a mile and a half, with Dover harbour now close in front and below, you will get the choice a bearing left along a broad shoulder around the cliff, or going ahead up fenced steps. Go up the steps.
- Follow the fence to reach a kissing gate in 100 yards. Do not go through the gate but pass above it, keeping the fence on your left, with a radar tracking station just up the slope to the right.
- Pass through a kissing gate, with the fence of the tracking station just on your right. The harbour is plainly in sight below you.
- Follow the path as it leads into a National Trust car park. Walk through the car park, passing toilets on your right, to the entrance drive, and follow the drive out to a road.
- Keep straight on. In a few yards, where the road bends sharp right downhill, keep straight on onto a footpath. Dover Castle is clearly seen in front of you.

*Dover Castle has been continuously occupied since the Iron Age. It is of vital strategic importance, commanding the port of Dover and the shortest sea crossing to Europe, and as such has been occupied and reinforced by successive invaders. The Romans occupied the old British hillfort here as early as 55BC, and after the invasion of AD43 soon built a massive fort here. They also built a lighthouse, to warn sailors of the presence of the cliff and the Goodwin Sands offshore. The bottom 20 feet of the Roman lighthouse can still clearly be seen beside the Saxon church within the castle walls. The Saxons built a fortified township on the site.*

*The present castle dates from Norman times and is one of the greatest examples of Norman military architecture in Britain. The castle was ordered by William the Conqueror immediately after the Conquest. It has a massive outer wall with 27 towers and a dry ditch cutting off the landward approaches, and a motte and bailey keep. The castle seen today is largely from the time of Henry II, who added an inner wall in 1180 with a further 14 towers. He also built the massive three-storey central keep and improved and strengthened the outer wall.*

*The castle has seen action several times: in 1216 it was defended for King John against Louis, Dauphin of France, it was captured by rebel barons during de Montefort's rebellion in 1265, and it was captured by parliament during the Civil War. But perhaps the greatest moment of the castle came in 1940. Beneath the castle there are a labyrinth of tunnels, started in 1797 as a bombardment-proof headquarters in the event of French invasion. They were greatly enlarged in the years leading up to 1939 and continuing up until 1943. These tunnels housed the headquarters of Coastal Command, containing telephone exchange, coding and cipher centre, operations rooms, a hospital and accommodation for headquarters staff and garrison. It was from here that Admiral Ramsay, commander of the Straits of Dover, organised the evacuation of 338,000 British and French soldiers from the beaches of Dunkirk in May 1940.*

**The castle, including the World War Two tunnels, Roman lighthouse and Saxon church, is open to the public from April to October, 10am–6pm, November to March, 10am–4pm. There is an admission charge, but it is free to members of English Heritage.**

- Descend steeply with the path, and soon go down some steps, passing to the left of a terrace of red-brick houses.
- At the foot of the steps, and at the end of the handrail on your left, do not follow a tarmacked path ahead but turn right onto an initially vague grassy path, with the hedges of gardens on your immediate right.
- Follow the path, keeping the A2 in its cutting close on your left hand and ignoring first a turn to the right and then one to the left.
- Follow the path through trees, now on a level with the A2.
- Bear right with the path and climb, finally up wooden sleeper steps, to a road.
- Turn left along the road and cross the A2 on a road bridge. Immediately over the bridge, turn right down some steps, following a footpath sign.
- Cross a stile and keep straight on up the right-hand edge of a field, with the A2 now on your right.
- At the end of the field exit via a gate. Do not turn right under the A2, but instead turn left through a gate and up a track.
- Follow the track through the farm to a road.
- Turn right along the road for a third of a mile to reach a roundabout.
- Go anticlockwise around the roundabout. Cross the A2 signed as 'Jubilee Way Dover' and continue to the next exit, the A258 Deal road.
- Go down the Deal road for 200 yards. Where the road bends, and just after a bend sign, turn right over a stile.
- Follow the left-hand field edge for 200 yards.

The vast keep of Dover Castle was largely
built during the reign of Henry II.

Radio masts have stood on this cliff since World War Two, when they provided a vital part of the nation's defences during the Battle of Britain. In August 1940 the RAF could put 749 aircraft into the skies, to oppose 2,550 German aircraft, and those aircraft had an endurance of little more than one hour. In that time they had to take off and gain sufficient height to intercept incoming enemy bombers and their escorts. To do this effectively, it was vital the fighters did not take off too early, or be put into the air to oppose a raid that was only a diversion. Radar stations such as the one here on Dover Cliffs played a vital part in supplying early and accurate information regarding the enemy's numbers and direction. The importance of these stations was recognised by the Germans, who on 12 August 1940 aimed huge raids specifically against radar installations, followed in the next four weeks by massive and near-continuous raids against RAF bases every day. On 15 September, in a desperate bid to break British resistance, the Luftwaffe turned its attentions to the terror bombing of London rather than concentrating upon defeating the RAF. This decision was the turning point in the Battle of Britain, for the switch to bombing the cities rather than airfields gave the RAF a vital respite. Had the Germans but known it, RAF losses in aircraft and especially in trained pilots were rapidly approaching crisis point. Although the Blitz of London and other cities continued until May 1941, the survival of the RAF was never again threatened, and with it the threat of invasion defeated.

Such was the ferocity of the aerial dogfights that took place in the skies above Dover Cliffs, as RAF Spitfires and Hurricanes battled to stop the German attack, that this area became known as 'Hellfire Corner'. By the time that the Battle of Britain ended in May 1941 England had lost 915 aircraft but had destroyed 1,733 enemy planes and forever blunted the Germans' capability of controlling the skies over Britain and with it the capacity to invade these shores.

- After 200 yards, cross a stile on the left and go along the right-hand edge of a field, passing between pillboxes.

The pillboxes are an eloquent reminder of the very real threat of invasion in 1940 and 1941. Designed as cheap gun-emplacements, thousands upon thousands of concrete pillboxes were pre-fabricated and erected very rapidly at all points where enemy forces could land, either by sea or from the air. The pillboxes had good all-round fields of fire from which the surrounding countryside could be commanded, and were sited to provide mutual support for each other. Each pillbox could be manned by only a very small handful of men. They were especially congregated in Kent, providing line after line of defensible positions from the coast to the outskirts of London, which would enable a fighting retreat, hugely costly to an invader, to be fought if necessary.

- At the end of the field cross a stile and pass through a patch of scrub to cross a second stile onto a T-junction of farm drives.
- Keep straight on up the drive opposite, passing the backs of barns on your right.
- Go through a gate and keep straight on up a grassy track for 10 yards to enter a field.
- Bear half-right across the field, making for the middle of woods seen ahead.

- On reaching the edge of the woods, bear half-left to continue along the right-hand edge of the field, now with a hedge and woods on your right.
- Where the woods turn away right, go quarter right across the next large field to reach a stile
- Cross the stile and go half-right across the next field, aiming for a stile in the fence.
- Cross this stile and bear quarter-left, to follow the bottom edge of the field, with a fence on your left.
- Follow the fence to a stile in the far corner of the field. Cross the stile and continue straight on along an enclosed track.
- At the end of the track, cross a stile and descend to the road. Turn right along the road to reach a T-junction.
- Turn right and follow the road into the village of St Margaret's at Cliffe. Ignore side turns, pass a garage on the left, and the Village Stores on your right. Fifty yards past the Village Stores, turn right up some steps into the churchyard.

*The Church of St Margaret of Antioch was built in the 12th century and remains virtually unaltered since then. It has a fine carved west door leading into an archaded nave which in turn leads through a splendid pointed arch into a wide chancel.*

*The church was twice hit during World War Two by shells, fired from France.*

*In 1696 a local farmer fell over the cliff and was mortally injured but survived long enough to bequeath money for a bell to be rung every evening during the winter months, to keep travellers away from the cliff edge. The tradition survives to this day.*

*The church has a Book of Remembrance for the sailors who died serving in the Dover Patrol. More recently, a window was installed in 1987 in remembrance of three local men who died on the* Herald of Free Enterprise *in Zeebrugge.*

- Pass through the churchyard, keeping the church on your left and passing an interesting late-Victorian family tomb behind the church. Follow the path out of the churchyard and back into the car park.

Printed in Great Britain
by Amazon